D0464950

The Future of Liberal Revolution

The Future of
Liberal Revolution

BRUCE ACKERMAN

Yale University Press   New Haven and London

Designed by Sonia Scanlon
Set in Joanna type by Rainsford Type, Danbury, Connecticut.
Printed in the United States of America by
Vail-Ballou Press, Binghamton, New York

Library of Congress Cataloging-in-Publication Data
Ackerman, Bruce A.
The future of liberal revolution / Bruce Ackerman.
p.   cm.
Includes index.
ISBN 0-300-05396-7 (alk. paper)
1. Europe, Eastern—Constitutional
law.   2. Justice, Administration of —Europe,
Eastern.   3. European federation.
4. Europe—Politics and government—1989–
I. Title.
KJC4445.A26   1992
320.947—dc20   92-24558
CIP

A catalogue record for this book is available
from the British Library.

The paper in this book meets the guidelines for permanence
and durability of the Committee on Production Guidelines
for Book Longevity of the Council on Library Resources.

10 9 8 7 6 5 4 3 2 1

Contents

Acknowledgments

I started scribbling in 1989 but didn't really put my ideas into shape until invited to give the Carl J. Friedrich Lecture at Harvard in the fall of 1990. Little remains from my talk that day. But it was a first step. Paul Starr and Steve Winter provided especially useful critiques.

I made my next and largest step the following year. A fellowship at the Wissenschaftskolleg in Berlin gave me time to think and to learn. This is one great place, full of interesting people and supportive staff. I was lucky that Stephen Holmes and Claus Offe decided to spend the academic year 1991–92 with me. Not only did they provide much insight, but Stephen connected me with the important network of Eastern European correspondents organized by the University of Chicago Law School's Center for the Study of Constitutionalism in Eastern Europe. I also learned a great deal from the critical reactions to my manuscript by others during their stay at the institute: Benjamin Barber, Amos Elon, Jon Elster, Peter Glotz, Rumyana Kolarova, Wolf Lepenies, Lolle Nauta, Wiktor Osiatynski, and Claudia Schmölders. They helped more than they know.

So did friends farther away: Bo Burt, Mirjan Damaška, Owen Fiss, George Fletcher, Paul Kahn, Juan Linz, Jerry Mashaw, Frank Michelman, Andrzej Rapaczynski, Jed Rubenfeld, Fritz Scharpf, Cass Sunstein, Harry Wellington. All of them provided thoughtful critiques of a draft, saving me from many mistakes and encouraging me to rethink the basic argument.

This reappraisal was presented in a series of lectures in

modern philosophy at the Institut für die Wissenschaften vom Menschen in Vienna. Once again, back to the drawing board, thanks to a remarkably informed and multifaceted critique. As I prepared the final revision, I was particularly helped by Spiros Simitis's perceptive commentary.

Important support was also provided long-distance from Yale. A Senior Faculty Fellowship helped with expenses. Mitch Lasser provided outstanding research assistance via fax and computer mail.

Through it all, my wife, Susan, was her usual self—friend, critic, lover, where would I be without you?

My essay "Die Zukunft der Liberalen Revolution" was published in 39 *Die Neue Gesellschaft/Frankfurter Hefte*, no. 3, 221–231 (March 1992). Material from it is scattered among the first three chapters of this book. An earlier version of the fourth chapter was published in German as "Von der Revolution zur Verfassung," in 4 *Transit* (1992).

Given the rapidly changing character of events, perhaps I should say that I closed the books on this book on June 15, 1992.

CHAPTER ONE

A New Era

From Warsaw to Moscow, Havana to Beijing, a specter haunts the world as if risen from the grave: the return of revolutionary democratic liberalism. This reappearance on the world stage has surprised liberals. Modern liberal thought has taken an antirevolutionary turn. Its proponents are unprepared to assimilate the meaning of the present historical moment.

One of Marxism's most consequential acts of appropriation in 1917 (or earlier) was to seize the idea of revolution. Of course, there were many more non-Marxist than Marxist revolutions even at the height of Leninism's ascendancy. But the Leninists were remarkably successful in getting nearly everyone to believe that their kind of revolution was the genuine article and that others were sham or worse. Only Hannah Arendt raised a powerful protest against this usurpation; and I follow her in suggesting that we must reassess the very idea of revolution before we can define its future.[1]

But there is a second stumbling block as well, which requires us to rethink liberalism no less than revolution. Twentieth-century liberals have been so traumatized by the struggle with Marxism and Nazism that they have adopted a steadfastly antirevolutionary stance. To reassert the centrality of revolution, I must confront the self-satisfied character of this conventional wisdom: Should "mature" Westerners reserve the idea of liberal revolution for lesser breeds emerging from tyranny? Are the Marxists right in this at least—that the age of liberal revolution has passed in the capitalist West? Or has it just begun?

The revolutions in Eastern Europe have done more than destroy the Soviet Union. They have thrown Western Europe into fundamental disequilibrium. For the first time in half a century, Western Europeans have begun to exercise full sovereignty over the basic conditions of their existence. As the United States retreats across the Atlantic, Europeans will become free to repeat the nationalist madness of the twentieth century. Forty-five years of peace have not eliminated the competitive European state system that caused the two great wars.

Unless decisive action is taken, the old sad story can repeat itself. It would be a tragic mistake to look upon 1989 as if it "merely" involved the end of the Cold War. It should instead be seen as part of a larger challenge. At present, Western European liberals are allowing nationalist groups to monopolize the arts of popular mobilization—while they continue with the techniques of elite political management that were so successful during the era of American hegemony. But is normal politics, as exemplified by the Maastricht agreements, adequate to the new situation? Before the old-fashioned balance of power generates new nationalist bitterness, should European liberals take the need for revolutionary mobilization seriously? Is it time for political elites to stop imagining that they can build a strong federal Europe without gaining the mass support of their fellow Europeans?

As we begin to take such questions seriously, a new perspective will open on another aspect of the emerging liberal order. Constitutionalism and the rule of law have been liberal watchwords for a long time. But once again, most recent discussions betray symptoms of the traumatic struggle with twentieth-century totalitarianisms. They focus on the protection of individual rights in a world on the brink of bureaucratic tyranny. This question is perennially important, and I have no interest in pushing it aside. Equally important now, however, is another, related question: How can constitutionalism allow revolutionary liberals to make the most of their opportunities and construct *enduring* forms of political order? The fate of revolutionary liberalism will depend on many things besides constitutional creativity; culture, economics, and geopolitics will make a tremendous difference. Nonetheless, the creative role of constitutionalism is easy to underestimate, and there is reason to fear that liberals are not fully exploiting its potential.

This is my thesis. I argue that the aftermath of revolution provides liberals with a special political opportunity. For a short time, successful revolutions characteristically generate a political constellation that allows for the mobilization of deep and broad support for a liberal constitution. If a postrevolutionary leadership takes advantage of this opportunity, its new constitution can shape the terms of political development for a long time to come. Without decisive leadership, the constitutional moment passes in vain.

Having glimpsed the urgency of constitutional construction, I next consider the paradoxical way in which other responses by the legal system may make the venture more difficult. Efforts to correct injustices perpetrated under the old regime raise the most troubling problem. These efforts may take a variety of forms, including criminal prosecution, publication of secret police files, and the return of private property seized by the Communists a generation or more ago. As a matter of principle, many of these claims will seem compelling. Nonetheless, the demand for justice, if given full play, can undermine the fragile political conditions for the powerful development of a liberal constitution. The better part of wisdom is to keep the demand for corrective justice under control while channeling energy toward the construction of an enduring constitutional order.

I then turn to consider the extent to which judges can realistically serve as guardians of liberal constitutions. America has the longest experience with the practice of judicial review. But on many matters, more can be learned from European models, especially the remarkable German experience with its Basic Law, enacted after the Hitler disaster. I conclude by returning to earlier themes: Do the revolutions of 1989 mark the end of history? Or do they open up a second age of liberal revolution that will change the face of Europe and the world?

This book is a high-risk project. Ten years from now, my hopeful talk of liberal revolution may seem ridiculous. But there has always been something ridiculous about liberal hopes, and yet they have somehow survived the horrors of the twentieth century. The question is whether the next century will be kinder—whether liberalism will thrive, not merely survive. Although the answer will depend on lots of things beyond human control, it will also depend on us, on our capacity to learn from the past and to create better governing structures for the future.

CHAPTER TWO

Rethinking Revolution

Revolution: the word has become one of the banalities of the late twentieth century. We have seen the story unfold so many times before; excited crowds, vague slogans, and charismatic leaders flicker on our television screens in a familiar sort of heroic (melo)drama. But surely we can think about it afresh. What makes revolution so engaging?

I begin with an abstract definition that encompasses Marxist revolutions in Russia, religious revolutions in Iran, nationalist revolutions in many places—as well as liberal revolutions. Only then can we see what, if anything, is distinctive about the last variety. We might also look for a concept capacious enough to encompass a broader family of phenomena, such as scientific revolutions. Where, then, to begin?

By remarking upon the distinctive revolutionary orientation to time. First and foremost, revolutionaries propose to cut time in at least two parts: a Before and a Now.[1] Before, there was something deeply wrong with the way people thought and acted. Now, we have a chance to make a "new beginning" by freeing ourselves from these blinders.

How does this new beginning occur? Through a collective act by mobilized and self-conscious participants. These men and women recognize the validity of new truths and practices—paradigms, if you will[2]—and proceed to reorganize their collective life by giving new weight to their importance. To put the definition in a single line: A revolution is a successful effort to transform the governing principles and practices of a basic aspect of life through an act of collective and self-conscious mobilization.

Note the absence of a key word: I do not insist that a movement induce a *total* change in governing principles to qualify as revolutionary.[3] To do so would demand the impossible. Rhetorical excess notwithstanding, there never has been, and never will be, a "total" revolution of all practices at once. Liberal revolutionaries in particular insist upon fundamental limitations on transformative ambition. To the few remaining totalists, these limitations make the liberal's revolutionary pretensions absurd.

But I see no reason to allow a few extremists to make revolution an impossible concept. In other areas of life, we regularly talk of revolutions without requiring a complete break in continuity. We speak, for example, of scientific revolutions without supposing that Copernicus broke with all his predecessors' principles. Nor do we expect revolutionaries in science to move beyond their domain and try to revolutionize music or sports.

So, too, with political revolutionaries: it is enough if they make big changes in the political system without transforming every sector of society. For example, I will consider a change from laissez-faire to a welfare state revolutionary—so long as it is achieved through self-conscious mass mobilization; similarly, an environmental revolution may well be in our future, even though many familiar practices will remain more or less the same.

This clarification still allows us to insist that not all big changes come through revolutions. Many, perhaps most, come through evolution.* Slowly, without anybody thinking much about the ramifications, a lot of changes add up. But accepting the reality of evolutionary change does not diminish the impact of revolutionary mobilizations upon modern life. How, then, do liberal revolutions differ from other kinds?

Three Types of Revolution, Two Types of Liberalism

We have been living with revolution for a long time. In both ancient Israel and classical Rome some people set themselves, and their own era, apart from all that preceded them by making a collective effort at a new beginning.[4] And, of course, it is impossible to understand Christianity without confronting the time-splitting consequences of Jesus' intervention in human history. What else divides the New Testament from the Old but a revolutionary break in time? Fundamentalist movements throughout the Islamic world make it plain that the age of religious revolution has not come to an end.

Nonetheless, most modern revolutions have been more secular. There are two types. The first is romantic: participants are urged to find new meaning in the language, practices, and symbols of a national culture.[5] Competing with romantic nationalism is a more rationalist type. Here the new beginning is attempted by participants who commit themselves to critical philosophical and scientific principles that they believe withstand rational scrutiny.

---

*For example, the Industrial Revolution is a revolution only in a metaphorical sense. James Watt didn't get together with other inventor-entrepreneurs and decide to inaugurate a new era. In contrast, George Washington and Lech Walesa did make this effort at collective and self-conscious mobilization.

I am dealing in ideal types. Revolutionaries may mix rationalistic, romantic, and religious themes into numberless combinations. Nonetheless, different historical revolutions have placed different emphases on these distinctive dimensions. To rehabilitate romantic nationalism, for example, I would draw my cautionary tales from Nazi Germany; to rehabilitate religious transformation, I would draw them from Iran. Because I will be defending the continuing importance of liberal revolutions of the rationalist type, my cautionary tales come from Marxism. It is the extravagant oppressions by the Leninist party that have given rationalist revolution a bad name.

So let me say what was wrong with Marxism-Leninism from a liberal-revolutionary point of view. First, its science of revolution was normatively impoverished. Rather than organizing their thought and program around critical principles of justice, Leninists believed that the whole question of justice was unscientific, hence bad. Second, Leninists tried to displace critical reflection on norms with a science of history that was beyond human understanding. Third, and unsurprisingly, given its grandiose aims, Leninist science turned out to be hideously wrong. Its predictions of postrevolutionary improvement were mocked by the reality of bureaucratic tyranny. Fourth, Leninists remained unrepentant in their scientistic pretensions, condemning those with false consciousness to harsh death or unspeakable humiliation. Fifth, the Leninist party was increasingly dominated by cynical opportunists without any real commitment to the rationalistic project of social transformation that had earlier motivated the revolutionary enterprise.

The hollowness of this failure is now apparent to all. The only question concerns the lesson we should learn from it: Should we try to save the idea of rationalist revolution from the historical debris or cheer its demise?

The answer is easy for those who treat liberalism as a synonym for laissez-faire capitalism. This understanding does have some support in historical practice and philosophical theory. Nineteenth-century liberals were sometimes single-minded in their celebration of free markets. Contemporary thinkers like Friedrich Hayek and Robert Nozick have been vigorous in urging a revival of this tradition.[6] It would be wrong to deny the existence of this laissez-faire strand of thought.

But it would be even wronger to give undue prominence to this nineteenth-century view. At least since John Stuart Mill and Thomas Hill Green, modern liberals have been trying to put the market in its place—as one, but only one, of a series of fundamental commitments. This effort now has its own century-long history, moving from John Dewey through John Rawls to a new generation of theorists who seek to sustain the ideals of activist liberalism. Broadly speaking, activists place four kinds of limitation on the operation of the free market. The first—expressed in a theory of market failure—emphasizes how real-world markets fail to conform to ideal models of perfect competition. This point, when elaborated, justifies a wide range of ongoing state interventions, from environmental control to consumer protection to the subsidized provision of old-age and health insurance.[7] The second—expressed in a theory of distributive justice—challenges the right of one generation of winners in the marketplace to pass economic gains to their children without providing equal opportunity for children who were unlucky enough to have poor parents.[8] The third—expressed in a theory of the material and cultural conditions for freedom—emphasizes the crucial importance of education in preparing each citizen for the exercise of meaningful choice.[9] The fourth—expressed in a theory of equal citizenship—assures all citizens roughly equal political resources despite their different fates in the marketplace.[10] Only within this larger framework—call it a structure of undominated equality—do activist liberals affirm the enduring value of the free market. Without constant efforts to approximate undominated equality, talk of a free market degenerates into an ideological apologia for the rich and powerful.

Perhaps this conclusion is not news for democratic socialists, who continue to look upon "capitalism" with suspicion. But unlike them, I am enthusiastic about the free market ideal. So long as people are guaranteed undominated equality, they have a fundamental right to trade with one another on terms that make sense to them. The challenge for the activist liberal state is to achieve structural conditions for the legitimate marketplace, not to destroy the genuine freedom that the market makes possible.

These are large and controversial claims, which I have defended elsewhere.[11] My aim here is to build a bridge between these activist ideals and liberal revolution. To put the matter simply, laissez-faire liberals like Hayek can think of only one possible role for revolution. It is a moment of the mobilized transition from an autocratic regime to a laissez-faire government that contents itself with protecting private property and freedom of contract. Although activist liberals recognize this new beginning as a moral triumph over the false claims of autocracy, they do not suppose that it represents the end of history. A laissez-faire system allows vast concentrations of inherited wealth, on one side, and an uneducated, propertyless class, on the other. Systematic maldistribution of wealth makes a mockery of the ideal of equal political participation; it is also compatible with all kinds of market failure: cartelization, environmental degradation, the massive exploitation of consumer ignorance. Hayek notwithstanding, no sensible liberal should remain satisfied with such transparent injustices. Generations of mobilized effort—many more new beginnings—will be required before any Western society can begin to approximate the liberal ideal of undominated equality.

Rethinking the Antirevolutionary Argument

I have been trying to clear a conceptual space for revolution in the activist tradition of modern liberalism. Much more work must be done before liberal revolution might seem a plausible program in one or another society. I start by confronting the most sweeping objections to my proposal. Because modern liberal thought has been shaped by combat with Nazism and Communism, it bristles with arguments that seem to condemn all revolutions, whatever their inspiration.[12] Defenders of liberal revolution must, then, explain why familiar arguments against twentieth-century pathologies overextend themselves when taken to antirevolutionary extremes.

To make my case, consider how the fundamental aim of liberal revolution differs from that of its competitors. These rivals seek nothing less than the transformation of human nature: through a mobilized act of collective self-consciousness, they will create a New Soviet Man or some other grim equivalent.

Revolutionary liberals do not yearn for radical conversion. They aim to support the incredible diversity of human aspiration, not suppress it. The challenge is to work for social justice in the distribution of opportunities for individual growth and development. A key interest is in the existing maldistribution of resources—in the fact that the millionaire's child has so many more chances to prosper than the ghetto kid. Other activists emphasize how unregulated markets generate large-scale environmental disasters or how competitive conditions can degenerate into monopolistic cartels. If a liberal citizenry is serious about correcting such structural injustices, it can succeed only if it is willing to undertake a generation-long effort at political mobilization aiming for a new beginning.

A major move toward undominated equality would require fundamental changes in Western society as we know it. But its partisans would abhor all attempts to use state power to coerce human beings into some narrow political mold. Whatever the failings of liberal revolutionaries, they cannot be accused of sharing the totalitarian ambition that has cursed twentieth-century transformations.

But we have only begun to define the future of liberal revolution. Obviously, the rich and powerful will not calmly hand over the unfair advantages they now enjoy and propose to pass on to their children. Isn't it more likely that they will fight on behalf of the status quo? Won't the ensuing bloodbath mock the modern liberal's utopian effort to reconcile liberty and equality?

My answer rejects the premise of such questions: the Leninist equation of revolution with violence. The pathology of violence unquestionably arises from the dynamics of the revolutionary enterprise itself. But once we understand its causes, need they overwhelm us? The temptation to violence arises because all revolutions begin with a small number of true believers who inevitably encounter resistance as they spread the word to others. This larger audience may be unpersuaded of the need for a new beginning. Rather than accepting the liberal's activist program, skeptics may look upon it as a cover for less noble motives: Isn't "undominated equality" just a fancy way of describing envy and greed?

At this point, revolutionary arrogance becomes tempting. So far as the vanguard is concerned, the resisters are victims of false consciousness. If the recalcitrant exercised their critical intelligence, they would find themselves convinced of the need for a new beginning; only sloth or selfishness or worse is keeping them back. So why not force them to be free; later on they will be grateful for the therapy.

The liberal revolutionary rejects this gambit. Violence is not a necessary condition for the mobilization of critical self-consciousness. After all, the vanguard itself grasped the need for revolutionary change through the force of argument, not the force of weapons. Why give up hope that years of committed political activity will lead others—many others—to respond to persuasion?

Violence is simply a shortcut, and one that should be

avoided in the name of liberal values themselves. Men and women have the right to be wrong, even about social justice. They have a right to demand that would-be revolutionaries take their objections seriously, that the revolutionaries persuade, not coerce, them to rework their ideals of the good society. The examples of Gandhi and King establish that such a generation-long struggle can yield results that are more profound and sustaining than the quick kills of a Lenin or a Hitler. Perhaps violence may be justified as a last resort, if the power elite responds to liberal demands for social justice by brutally suppressing the revolutionary movement. But it is far, far better if we respond to vanguardism—the arrogance of the counterelite—by designing a constitutional system that subjects would-be revolutionaries to a series of fair democratic tests.

Constitutionalizing Revolution?

This is the aim of a distinctively "dualistic" form of liberal constitutionalism. Basic to the dualist's design is the construction of a two-track lawmaking system.[13] The lower lawmaking track is intended to register the successful conclusions of pluralist democratic politics—the mix of interest group pressure, regular electioneering, and practical policymaking that characterizes the democratic polity most of the time.

The higher lawmaking track, in contrast, is designed with would-be revolutionaries in mind. It employs special procedures for determining whether a mobilized majority of the citizenry give their considered support to the principles that one or another revolutionary movement would pronounce in the people's name. Although many small movements feel themselves called to the task of revolutionary renewal, dualists emphasize that few are chosen by a mobilized majority of a nation's citizens. Hence, the higher lawmaking system imposes a rigorous set of institutional tests before allowing a revolutionary movement to transform fundamental political principles. The most basic test is the passage of time. Before a revolutionary change is adopted, it should have the sustained support of a substantial majority, not just support at a single moment.

But the mere passage of time is not enough. Before an initiative deserves enactment, it should gain support that is qualitatively different from that given to normal legislation. Popular debate must be given full play before a final decision is reached. Both partisans and opponents should be guaranteed a fair chance to muster nationwide backing. The dualist aims for more than a mechanical vote-count at a referendum. The higher lawmaking system is intended to determine whether a revolutionary initiative has gained the considered support of a self-conscious and deliberate majority.

Once a self-proclaimed vanguard subjects itself to such onerous tests, it will often find itself exposed as the voice of a small minority. But this is by no means inevitable. After long years of work, a revolutionary movement may traverse the obstacle course established by the higher lawmaking system. If it does so, the dualistic constitution gives the call for a new beginning special status in the legal system. Until the next successful revolution, the new principles will serve as higher law and will trump the outcomes of normal politics.

This two-track system is not an unseasoned idea. To the contrary, it helps account for the remarkable endurance of the United States Constitution over the past two centuries.

The longevity of the Constitution is often seen as testimony to the stability of American society—but mistakenly so. When the Constitution was formulated in 1787, America was a thinly settled former colony. Before the new nation became the leading economic and military power of the world, it underwent a series of transformations—from the slaveocracy of 1787 to the market capitalism prominent after the Civil War, from the laissez-faire of the early twentieth century to the welfare state of the New Deal, from the token equality of yesterday to the contemporary effort to assure more genuine equality for blacks and women.

The reason why the American Constitution could incorporate such revolutionary changes lies in the founders' decision to endow it with a distinctive two-track structure. Before political leaders are constitutionally empowered to embark on transformations in fundamental principles, they are required to prove that they have earned the mobilized and self-conscious support of the People by successfully meeting the obstacles prescribed by the higher lawmaking system. They are not permitted to manipulate the lower lawmaking system in the ordinary way of parliamentary democracy.

Perhaps a thought experiment will clarify the special role of higher lawmaking in the United States. The American Civil War was one of the bloodiest struggles that the world experienced between 1815 and 1914. If such a bloodbath had occurred elsewhere, it is perfectly possible that the victorious Republicans might have followed the French example by proclaiming the existence of a Second Republic that repudiated the First Republic's guarantee of the master-slave relationship.

But the Americans took a different path. They tried to use the special system of constitutional amendment left by the founders to structure the debate and decision over the meaning of their new beginning. Instead of attempting a total break with the past, the Republicans sought to adapt the inherited higher lawmaking system to gain public credibility for their claim that the majority of the American people had given their self-conscious and considered support to their revolutionary principles of emancipation and equal citizenship.

A similar approach to revolutionary change marks America's twentieth-century experience. Neither Franklin Roosevelt nor Martin Luther King, Jr., aimed to destroy the legal system to mobilize public support for the transformation from laissez-faire to the welfare state or from Jim Crow to interracial equality. The dualistic constitution provided them with the legal resources to consolidate their peaceful revolutions. These successes stand out from the many false starts in American history. Far more often, a political vanguard calls for a new beginning only to discover that a majority of the people refuse to go along.

But this is not the place to explore the historical details.[14] The important point is more abstract. Once we loosen the Marxist-Leninist grip on the idea, there is nothing odd about the thought of a *peaceful* democratic revolution. Not only do the Eastern European events of 1989 emphasize this possibility, but the American system of dualistic democracy helps give it constitutional reality. By establishing a special system for higher lawmaking, a dualistic constitution provides revolutionary vanguards with an alternative to fierce battles in the streets. Rather than glorifying force, it encourages them to submit their cause to the onerous tests imposed on revolutionary proposals by the higher lawmaking system.

Some revolutionaries will reject this invitation. But then they should be treated as the thugs that they are. Rather than embracing force, liberal revolutionaries reject violence; they support a dualistic structure that reliably controls vanguardism in the name of genuinely popular deliberation and decision.[15]

Revolution and the Limits of Reason

So far, I have been considering two moral questions: Does revolution require the radical transformation of human nature? Does it compel the brutal celebration of violence? If so, liberals are well rid of their nineteenth-century illusions about the promise of revolution. If not, we can take another step down the path of exploration.

Suppose, for a moment, that a majority of liberal citizens mobilized themselves to support a new beginning in which their country pledged itself to the serious pursuit of genuine equality of opportunity or systematic environmental protection. If this commitment were made, would liberals know enough to devise a set of state interventions that will do more good than harm? Wouldn't their best-laid plans be swamped by second-order effects that mocked the ideals motivating the revolutionary enterprise? Isn't the world too complex for our puny efforts at social engineering to succeed? Shouldn't we recognize the revolutionary demand for principled transformation as the delusion that Hayek says it is: a phantasm that authorizes technocrats to impose a rigid tyranny upon the rest of us?[16]

Although laissez-faire ideologists may treat these questions as rhetorical, the student of revolution should examine case studies seriously. For now, it is enough to glance at American history. Two centuries ago, the revolutionaries who instituted the Constitution thought they possessed a political science sufficiently powerful to establish a new form of republican government. A lot has happened since, but are we prepared to say that they failed?

More than a century ago, Americans fought a war to free the slaves; and at the end of the war, the slaves were freed. Modern Americans may say that their predecessors' notion of freedom was impoverished, but that is a very different point from the skeptical claim that revolutions cannot achieve their professed aims.

Here are a couple of more recent cases. The New Deal revolution aimed to establish protection against the vagaries of old age, accident, disability, and unemployment. Today, many Americans have social security, thanks to this collective act of self-conscious political mobilization. The civil rights movement aimed to end apartheid in the American South and to provide more genuine opportunities for oppressed races. To ignore civil rights successes may be fashionable in some circles, but in fact, Americans have ended apartheid and minorities have won more genuine opportunities.

I do not want to play Pangloss. A lot is wrong with American public arrangements, and even more, with Americans' limited ambition. The American people have not yet been convinced to embrace the full promise of social justice in a liberal state, much less to make it a living reality. This is exactly why I want to reject the Marxist myth that the age of liberal revolution has long since passed in the "capitalist" West. My only point is this: American history does not justify the kind of radical skepticism about the possibility of self-conscious social change that is trendy in neoconservative circles.[17]

Despite all the ironies of history, revolutionaries have, over the past two centuries, often achieved some of their central aims. Many of these revolutionary "successes" have yielded great evils: Stalin's collectivization, Hitler's final solution. But this is because many of the successful revolutions of the twentieth century have been antiliberal. We may despair at the instrumental success of antiliberal revolutions, but not at the failure of the revolutionaries to attain their goals. Why should liberals surrender the idea of mobilized political change to their opponents?

Although conservatives have long doubted the liberal capacity to master the arts of social engineering, a new kind of doubt has gained prominence over the past decade. These skeptics also scrutinize the theory of knowledge underlying liberalism. But they do not concern themselves with the daunting empirical inquiries that liberals confront in designing programs for the real world. The new doubt goes deeper— to the liberal's theory of moral knowledge.

The rising critique, often described as communitarian, challenges the liberal idea of personhood.[18] The liberal's demand for social justice makes no sense, communitarians say, without positing the existence of abstract and isolated Egos who are scarecrows of the real-world folks we know and love. Although a few philosophers may be convinced by abstruse Kantian texts to accept these alienated Egos as the key to personal identity, communitarians are confident that most people are repelled by such a forbiddingly antiseptic construction. Whatever neo-Kantians may say, most people simply do not think of themselves as Abstract Choosers whose dignity consists in the possession of Equal Rights. Ordinary humans gain their identity by sharing in the preexisting commitments and traditions of their community. Why, then, should they sacrifice themselves when the liberal revolutionary calls upon them to join together to guarantee equal rights for all?

I leave this question to my allies who see the deepest expression of political liberalism in Kant's philosophy.[19] I myself have never been a member of the Kantian party. Indeed, most liberals of the past have rejected the Kantian image of an abstract and isolated Ego. They have emphasized the profound ways that human identity is bound up with the body, the senses, and each individual's experience of society. However different Locke, Hume, Mill, and Dewey are from one another, they are alike in their rejection of the Kantian theory of the self. Only a shallow critique awards Kant an intellectual monopoly he has never possessed in modern liberal thought.

If pressed for a counterformulation, I would say that the creature haunting my own thought is not the deracinated self but the flesh-and-blood person that we call a stranger. Strangers may live next door, but they are not like us. They are doing odd things at odd times for reasons that disturb us in basic ways.

How to respond to this unease?[20] By loving the strangers as ourselves? Only a god could do this: there are too many strangers with too many strangenesses. Or should we persuade the strangers to change their actions and beliefs so that they agree with ours? I would never give up on this project.

But persuasion and reflection take time; I must listen to the strangers' arguments if I expect them to listen to mine. In the meantime, an abyss lies between us, and we may die before one of us comes to see the other's truth for what it is.

How, then, are we to conduct our ongoing life together? Are we forever fated to repeat the mistake of the ancient Greeks, who despised others as barbarians merely because their talk sounded like *bar, bar, bar* to Greek ears? Must we endlessly destroy what we cannot understand? No, there is an alternative: we must try to become politically self-conscious about the very problem posed by our continuing strangeness and try to construct a political solution. You and I may remain strangers, but we may find common ground in a politics that protects our equal right to cultivate our distinctive characters without any one stranger calling the shots.

By working with one another to build a liberal state dedicated to our equal right to be different, we may become something more than strangers, if less than friends. We may become liberal citizens, speaking to one another in a distinctive voice. However odd or perverse our beliefs may seem to one another, perhaps we can find common ground in recognizing this: you and I are both struggling to find meaning in the world. We can—we must—build a civilized political life that allows each of us to respect the others' quest.

This is the promise of liberal revolution. I do not encounter you in some mythic state of nature but in the here and now. I ask you to work with me to shape a world that gives equal respect to our right to be different. By working out a public understanding of the practical implications of this idea, we may inaugurate a new beginning in our relationships with one another. We may succeed so well that our children, looking back, will say: Thanks to them, we have come to give new significance to the proud boast that all men are created equal.

Or we may fail. Liberal revolution is hard work—harder than the revolutionary exercises proposed by religious and nationalist rivals, who can offer a deep spiritual satisfaction that liberals deny themselves. These rivals allow their devotees to proclaim, in a variety of accents: We are the Chosen Ones, let the rest of humanity go to hell.

Liberal revolutionaries cultivate a principled split between public and private personas. Publicly, they call out to their confreres to join together to build a political life of mutual respect and civility. Privately, they may find that their public encounters only confirm their doubts about the ethical ideals held by the strangers they greet as fellow citizens. The tension between private conviction and public tolerance will be difficult to bear. Using state power to suppress difference is so much easier than supporting or enduring it.

But managing this spiritual tension is only part of the problem. The practical challenges of liberal statecraft raise special difficulties. Other revolutionaries may flirt with totalizing conceptions of the state, using central power to project their religious or national Idea into the furthest recesses of social life. The liberals' relation to the state is more complex. On the one hand, they must use centralized power creatively to guarantee each citizen a fair share of basic resources—health, wealth, education—as he or she sets out in the quest for meaning. On the other hand, they embrace the principle of limited government. It is not the job of the state to answer the fundamental questions of life, but to equip all individuals with the tools they need to take responsibility for their own answers.

This double-edged commitment generates a characteristic search to define a limited set of strategic state interventions to secure initial equality. Progressive taxation and compulsory primary education serve as classic examples. The challenge is to define new forms of intervention that will make undominated equality a social reality. As fundamental entitlements are secured, the liberal legal order seeks to provide citizens with a broad set of facilitative tools, such as freedom of contract and freedom of association, so they can trade and collaborate on their own terms within a just basic structure.

This program commits the liberal revolutionary to the rule of law. Citizens should not be obliged to kowtow before bureaucrats. The law *guarantees* them fundamental rights to an equal starting point in life and offers a rich set of techniques for collaboration. And it is the job of judges to interpret this law, not appeal to their own private notions of moral perfection in resolving disputes. Revolutionary justice, in short, is provided by a rule of law that effectively guarantees all citizens their equal right to be different.

All this is easier said than done. But I do not apologize for beginning in this moralistic way. If the idea of liberal revolution is a bad one in principle, we should stop at the threshold and not waste any more time on it. If it remains a serious option, our argument should take a more pragmatic turn.

CHAPTER THREE

The Next European Revolution

The revolutions of 1989 have generated enormous commentary, but few have suggested that Westerners might learn something fundamental about their own political prospects. The learning curve apparently goes in one direction—from west to east. Although Jürgen Habermas and Francis Fukuyama are poles apart, both agree that the West has nothing to learn from the "catch-up" revolutions in the East, except perhaps that the West has reached the "end of history."[1]

We won, you lost, and it's about time that the East catches up. I suppose that an orgy of self-congratulation is natural after so much Cold War tension. More puzzling is the way that Eastern Europeans are ratifying the derivative character of their revolutions. Of course, they have better things to do with their time than suggest that they are the first wave of a larger liberal transformation. But more than modesty or distraction is at work: the roots of Eastern diffidence can be traced to Marxist structures of thought inherited from the past.

Whatever the intellectual roots of this emerging consensus, I mean to challenge it. The year 1989 can and should serve as the beginning of an era in which liberals again walk the world with a sense of revolutionary opportunity. Because politics is the art of the possible, I make my point concrete by reconsidering emerging realities in Western Europe. I ask, How might liberals mobilize mass support for a revolutionary transformation of the old state system that has led to repeated disasters in the twentieth century?

I will not plunge into this question immediately but will try to locate it within the larger context of theory and practice that has accumulated since the first age of liberal revolution. Only within this larger context does it make sense to consider the potential contribution of 1989 to the ongoing effort to define the range of political possibility.

Theory and Practice

Liberal revolutions differ systematically from those attempted by more religious or romantic types. For these rivals, the revolutionary moment can be a time when the masses are most alive to the national and religious ideals that make life worth living. Naturally enough, these revolutionaries want their time of triumph to go on indefinitely. As a consequence, they are often fascinated with the idea of permanent revolution.

For activist liberals, matters stand differently. The revolutionary moment is indeed a time when citizens are most alive to their problem in political construction: How, given fundamental disagreements, are they to elaborate principles of justice that will give all a fair and equal opportunity to pursue their different lives? These moments are precious in the life of the polity. They allow its members to renew and redefine a common political identity that may otherwise be drowned out in a cacophony of different voices. Nonetheless, even the most revolutionary crisis should never entirely displace the task each of us faces in responding to the simple question: What is the meaning of my life? Some liberal activists will find the answer in a lifelong dedication to public service, but they cannot be surprised when others turn away from politics in quest of meaning elsewhere—in religion, philosophy, art, science, love and kindness, the business of life.

Liberal revolutions are passing events. During these periods of mass engagement, citizens place the problem of political reconstruction at the forefront of their consciousness, seeking to do justice to the problems thrown up by their historical situation. The challenge for statecraft is to use these fleeting moments to build new and stronger foundations for liberal politics, before the opportunity for self-conscious transformation is lost in the centrifugal whirl of liberal society.[2]

In the best case, a liberal state will experience a distinctive cycle of revolutionary activity over the generations. At one time, a mobilized citizenry will focus its attention upon the political problem posed by their differences and will mobilize themselves to frame appropriate principles of constitutional justice. If they succeed, most citizens then direct most of their energies elsewhere, leaving the adaptation and implementation of these principles to electorally responsible politicians and legalistically inclined judges. As normal politics proceeds, the proud constitutional principles of the previous revolutionary period suffer ossification. New forms of difference become central in social life; new historical conditions throw the older revolutionary principles into doubt. Finally, a new generation senses a need to transform old vocabularies, confront existing differences, and create a new liberal order that does justice to their self-conscious scrutiny. If revolutionary renewal succeeds, political mobilization will subside, for the collective revolutionary achievement empowers most people to explore their differences, rather than their commonalities.

But, to put it mildly, the liberal cannot count on the Invisible Hand to lead the revolutionary enterprise down the historical path to the best case. During the past two centuries, the idea of revolution has swept the world, leaving diverse experiences in its wake. These different experiences have had a profound impact upon political memory. Some political cultures have come to look upon the revolutionary aspect of their history with fear and loathing; others, with hope and expectation.

A thoughtful assessment of liberal revolution cannot ignore the way these historical memories can shape the future.[3] In parts of the world, the experience of revolution has left behind a bitter residue of cultural suspicion. The first proto-modern historical experience—the English revolution of the seventeenth century—had this effect. After a generation of bloody conflict, English revolutionaries saw their hopes for a new beginning destroyed by the Restoration of 1660. From that moment to the present, English political culture has expressed a pervasive suspicion of the constructive possibilities of self-conscious mobilization—an almost visceral belief that the noisy excitement of revolutionary politics leads to demagogic irrationality, not moral seriousness or rational engagement on matters of political principle.

Revolution in Germany has had the same fate: there has been one failure after another, capped by the nationalist madness of the Nazis. After 1848 and 1933, German liberals, and not only liberals, respond to tremors of mass mobilization with unconcealed anxiety. The very notion that a mass movement might lead to rational political reconstruction seems almost a utopian dream. From this perspective, the recent upheaval in East Germany is a matter of the greatest importance. Will it lead to a new confidence in the constructive possibilities of revolution or to deepened despair?

We shall see. My point is cautionary. Because modern liberal thought is so indebted to the English and German traditions, many of its proponents abhor revolution. The liberal skepticism of a Michael Oakeshott or a Friedrich Hayek expresses in part the failures of self-conscious mass mobilization in England and Mitteleuropa.

In many places, however, the revolutionary exercises of the past play a central and affirmative role in the self-definition of a political culture. Although many colonial revolutions were not firmly rooted in a mobilized and self-conscious citizenry, some were sufficiently grounded in the popular consciousness to serve as crucial elements in national political identity. No matter how different India, Mexico, Israel, and Turkey may be, they are the same in this: an affirmative valuation of a modern episode of revolutionary mobilization plays a crucial role in their political self-definition. None of these cases fits neatly into the ideal type of rationalistic liberal revolution that I have been constructing. Nonetheless, liberal revolutionaries in these and other places may well make imaginative use of indigenous precedents and symbols as they struggle to push history in a progressive direction.

A colonial revolution that comes closer to the ideal type is the first successful one in the modern world—in the English colonies of North America in the late eighteenth century. I have already suggested that the American revolutionaries not only succeeded in their own terms by beating the British, establishing a constitution, and then maintaining themselves in power with popular support for the remainder of their lives. They also established models of legitimate revolutionary activity that shaped the theory and practice of subsequent generations, for better and for worse. The dominant national narrative invariably emphasizes the positive contributions of revolutionary mobilization to American national identity: Abraham Lincoln speaking for the victorious Republicans of Reconstruction, Franklin Roosevelt for the New Deal Democrats, and Martin Luther King, Jr., for the civil rights movement stand for the best in the ongoing revolutionary tradition of activist liberalism.[4]

It is not necessary to leave Europe to find favorable self-evaluations of the revolutionary project. Like the Americans, the French look back to their eighteenth-century revolution as the great new beginning of their history. They are constantly finding exemplary significance in one or another of its achievements. The Declaration of the Rights of Man and Citizen, no less than the American Constitution, symbolizes the good that mobilized and self-conscious political action can accomplish. Yet the American and the French experiences also display fundamental differences. Most important, the revolutionary generation in France failed to achieve a stable success. A person whose political maturity came with the storming of the Bastille lived to see the Terror, Napoleon, and the Bourbon Restoration mock the liberal ideals that inspired the Declaration of Rights. During the same period, an American would have seen a succession of revolutionary heroes from Washington to Monroe demonstrate the continuing vitality of his generation's political achievement. The failure of the French to institutionalize their revolutionary moments in 1830 and 1848 casts a further shadow on their political thought, making it more pessimistic about the possibilities of enduring political reconstruction than its American counterpart.

And yet, despite the historical failure to stabilize their regime, French revolutionaries created powerful positive symbols that remain central to European political identity. Although Leninists managed to appropriate these symbols during much of the twentieth century, contemporary historians have shown how much Marxist mythology has distorted the past.[5] The challenge for activist liberals in Europe is to reassert the lost promise of the French Revolution and develop a modern vocabulary that, without denying the blunders and tragedies of the past, affirms the need for Europeans to fulfill that promise.

The Revolutions of 1989

Within this framework, the revolutions of 1989 represent a spiritual challenge. Will they be viewed as local events with little enduring significance? Or will they provoke the rest of us to take seriously the promise of liberal revolution?

The initial response has tended in the trivializing direction. Although the self-satisfaction of Westerners does not require elaborate explanation, the reticence of Easterners is more puzzling. Why have they failed to suggest that Western liberals might profit from their example in revolutionary mobilization? Perhaps because the Marxist legacy continues to shape the thought of most Eastern European intellectuals, despite their emphatic efforts at liberation?

To test this hypothesis, consider that many of the most arresting insights won by Eastern European thinkers during the 1980s were strikingly "antipolitical," to use Gyorgy Konrad's term.[6] The emphasis was not upon elaboration of an affirmative vision of the liberal state but on the need to maintain personal integrity in the daily encounter with a corrupt and bureaucratized Marxism. The most enduring images were provided by Vaclav Havel, whose calls to "live in the truth" evoke the best of the liberal spirit in opposition to the oppressive banalities of bureaucratic totalitarianism.

These calls for existential integrity are not nearly enough, however, to define the challenges of politics after the revolution—when the state will not wither away, but must be reorganized to support an open and just society. From this vantage, living in the truth can be positively dangerous, at least if the truth is understood with grim philosophical passion. For liberals, the problem with the Communist effort to construct a New Soviet Man goes beyond the falseness of the vision. The objection challenges the very effort by politicians to impose their own ideal of the Truth upon the rest of us. The aim of liberal revolution is not collective truth but individual freedom—freedom for each person to assert his or her moral ideals, even if a neighbor considers them "wrong." So long as citizens respect each other's equal freedom to seek the truth, they have the fundamental right to reject the truths propounded by those in power.

They have this right even when the propounder of the truth is President Havel. I greatly admire Havel as a man, but I would be alarmed if he proposed to act on his more philosophical essays as president of his republic. In particular, I deny that Havel's philosophical hero, Martin Heidegger, provides the key to living in the truth. Indeed, I suspect that Heidegger's early and enthusiastic Nazism is an organic expression of his larger philosophy. Havel's recurring endorsement of Heideggerian contempt for the Enlightenment in general and Western consumerism in particular has an authoritarian ring.[7]

Truth to tell, I am not much worried about Havel acting out his dark musings. He is too decent a person to allow philosophical predilections to spin out of control. Indeed, as president, he has been particularly sensitive to the rights of unpopular groups, using his moral authority to defend them in ways that I find admirable.[8] Havel's anti-Enlightenment philosophy, however, will not make it easy for him to give intellectual expression to his liberal instincts. Whatever good he may do in Czechoslovakia, he will not challenge Westerners to take the possibility of liberal revolution seriously.

Havel is a special person, whose encounters with the realities of Marxism have generated a rather special philosophical response. Yet I fear that the thinking of many other Eastern Europeans will also be shaped by their encounter with Marxism—even though, unlike Havel, they often defend Enlightenment values in political debate. These Marxist residues will not rise to the surface of their speculations about political life. Many powerful voices condemn Marxist longings for the construction of a new personality type who can somehow successfully merge self-interest into the interest of whole. As an alternative, Eastern Europeans have developed a rich literature on "civil society," emphasizing the crucial need to construct institutional spaces that might serve as a buffer against the totalitarian pretensions of the state. The aim here is to describe a more modest kind of political involvement in which citizens can control the state without merging their identity into the collective whole.[9]

Nonetheless, Marxist thought-ways may survive on a more structural level as what I call inverted Marxism. In this neo-liberal pattern, as in the abandoned dogma, history is seen as an epic struggle between three large sociological entities—feudalism, capitalism, and socialism. Inverted Marxism differs from the old-fashioned variety simply in rooting for a different winner. Whereas Communists championed socialism, the neoliberals say that capitalism is the best place to get off the train of history—as in the famous joke that defines Communism as "the most painful transition from capitalism to capitalism."

But this is no joking matter. The inverted Marxist pattern carries forward three serious mistakes. The first error treats capitalism as if it were the name of a single alternative to communism. This "fallacy of the single alternative" denies the existence of a third way between capitalism and communism. Scoffing at a third way is now very popular, but the scoffers are effective only so long as we allow them to remain vague about what they mean by capitalism. Does this label describe Germany, with its elaborate welfare state and worker participation in industry? Or America, with its rigorous restrictions upon discriminatory employment practices and intrusive environmental controls on industry? Or Japan, with its aggressive state planning? Or Singapore, with its autocracy? Or a picture of laissez-faire England in the middle of the nineteenth century? Or the activist liberal's ideal of undominated equality?[10]

Given the Marxists' aim, it made sense for them to use *capitalism* as an umbrella term. After all, they were trying to convince us that all non-Communist systems were fundamentally bad. But it is wrong for liberal revolutionaries to carry over the capitalist label into their own thinking. Rather than rejecting capitalism for communism, we must recognize that there are many capitalisms, some much better than others.

The second error brought forward in inverted Marxism is economism—treating the ownership and organization of the means of production as the only question of consequence. This may be sufficient for Marxists, but it represents a radical misunderstanding of liberalism. Liberalism is not the same thing as capitalism, however defined. The liberal's first commitment is to a distinctive political culture—to a process of self-government in which citizens build a society that allows them to realize their personal ideals under conditions of freedom and equality. Private property and competitive markets, when properly regulated, serve as one element in this larger liberal ideal. If liberal revolutionaries do not give careful attention to other elements, they may needlessly smooth the path from capitalism to autocracy, monopoly, and mass impoverishment.

The third error indulges the "fallacy of the last revolution." As is well known, Marxists sometimes imagined that once a society made its great breakthrough from capitalism to socialism, no further revolutionary mobilizations were required on the way to utopia. The inverse Marxist continues this mistake by supposing that no future popular mobilizations will be required after the painful transition back to capitalism. This mistake is closely tied to the others. If there is only one capitalism, and if capitalism is the essence of liberalism, then the transition back to capitalism represents the last liberal revolution. Once we break this chain of stipulative definitions, the liberal future is far more open-ended than the inverse Marxist allows. The reintroduction of private property and free contract does indeed represent an important advance over bureaucratic tyranny. But this single breakthrough is only one of many that will be required to achieve an open society that is both free and just, or even decent.

Not that I expect my own version of activist liberalism to carry the day any time soon in Eastern Europe. Reacting against Marxism, many members of the present revolutionary leadership seem infatuated by the liberating power of the free market, leaving it to old-line Communists to pose as friends of the oppressed. Decades could pass before the social injustice and environmental damage of an unregulated marketplace will impress itself upon a new generation of Easterners, who will be in a position to formulate a critique of the marketplace in liberal, rather than Marxist, terms.

Liberal revolutions come in cycles. The ideal of undominated equality will not be achieved through a single great leap forward. Many more new beginnings will be needed before the moral promise of liberalism is exhausted by the political practice of any existing society. It is pointless, though, to speculate about the shape of the Eastern European revolution of 2020: the next generation will be very lucky if all it has to worry about is the consequences of its parents' overenthusiastic embrace of the free market.

The Next Revolution

Things stand differently in Western Europe. The challenge here is to break the bubble of self-congratulation generated in 1989 and grasp the revolutionary possibilities implicit in the emerging order. For the first time since World War II,

Western Europeans—especially citizens of the reunited Germany—will have to learn to govern themselves without the constant military and political intervention of the United States and the Soviet Union. How they respond to their newfound freedom will profoundly shape the political possibilities that seem realistic to the rest of us. Western Europe is the source of many of the liberal ideals and practices that struggle against more culturally entrenched authoritarianisms elsewhere in the world. As Europeans take increasing responsibility for their own political fate, will they use the opportunity, at long last, to realize the promise of their own liberal heritage?

Perhaps the anxiety of my question may seem misplaced. At no time in European history have liberal values seemed so dominant, or the need for revolutionary mobilization so remote. But appearances are deceiving. The present calm is largely the result of fifty years of limited sovereignty in Europe. Dominated by military hegemons and caught up in ideological confrontation, the "great powers" of Europe were in no position to continue the military-nationalist competition that generated such disastrous consequences from 1870 to 1945. As John Mearsheimer has brilliantly argued, however, the basic structure for renewed competition between Germany and the other European powers was only repressed, not destroyed, during the Cold War.* With the disintegration of the

---

*See John Mearsheimer, "Back to the Future: Instability in Europe after the Cold War," 15 *International Security* 5 (1990). I should add that Mearsheimer is very much a member of the hard-nosed realist school of international relations and barely considers the possibility of a revolutionary movement for a federal Europe as a serious response to the structural problems he locates. Instead, he is more interested in clever counterintuitive measures to amelio-

Soviet Union and the predictable retreat of the United States, Western Europe is at a crossroads. It may gradually succumb to the forces of a resurgent nationalism that, over a generation or two, may lead to mutual distrust, protective military reaction, and ultimate disaster. Or it may take advantage of this propitious moment to decisively transform the relation between the nation-state and the emerging structures of a federal Europe.

The revolutionary challenge to the nation-state proceeds on two fronts. Throughout Western Europe, there has been an increasing recognition that genuine cultural community is best expressed on the substate level. Beginning in Germany and Austria after World War II, a federalist wave has been slowly rolling through much of Western Europe. As part of the post-Franco settlement, Spain not only ceded significant power to the Basques and Catalans but also created a more general federal structure that enhances regional cultures throughout the country. During the 1980s, the French Socialists presided over a lesser but still significant decentralization that challenges centuries of bureaucratic centralism, while Belgium has gone very far indeed in federalist development.[11] Movements for regional political identity have also become important in Italy and the United Kingdom, although they have not yet undermined the claims of these nation-states to speak for reportedly unproblematic "national communities."

---

rate future tensions. For example, he favors the provision of nuclear arms for Germany as an appropriate way of maintaining peace within the new balance of power emerging in Europe. Such proposals only emphasize the need for more revolutionary thinking than Mearsheimer is willing to undertake.

As regionalisms proliferate from below, the nation-state has been increasingly constrained from above by a tightening web of legally binding relations to the "European" institutions—the Economic Community, a variety of transnational courts, and so forth. Thus far, the European institutions have not been the product of a popular movement to create a new beginning in political life on the Continent. They have been largely the work of political and economic elites, who have looked with distrust on revolutionary appeals to a common European identity. Operating against the background of the Cold War, these elites have been successful in managing a gradual evolutionary process; the agreements reached in Maastricht serve as the most recent stage in a very slow progress toward the distant goal of European federalism.

This reliance on elite-managed evolutionism has had important implications for the European system of political parties. Rather than building a transnational political movement for a democratic Community, Europeans have remained content with nation-centered party systems. Parties still speak to one another as if national politics were much more important than European politics. As a consequence perhaps, we often find very odd political conjunctions: the parties of the right have often been pro-European while the parties of the left have sometimes been quite skeptical of a capitalist version of Eurofederalism. These political conjunctions lead to a very dangerous possibility: the right could revert to its nationalist roots, and large elements on the left could remain skeptical. The evolutionary process, symbolized by Maastricht, could easily collapse as national politics turns emphatically nationalist.

Western Europe, in short, is in a state of potential disequilibrium. The challenge for liberals is to organize a mass movement for a federal Europe before retrograde nationalism spirals out of control. The choice is between nationalist reassertion and federalist construction. Liberals cannot afford to wait on the sidelines while nationalists indulge in populist demagogy. They must themselves become revolutionaries. Now is the time to transform the Europe of states into a Europe of cultural regions.

The link between Continentalism and regionalism is no marriage of political convenience. Something about federalism loves liberalism. If, as I have suggested, liberals insist on the need to deal with strangers with respect, this need is never so exigent as in a federation. If the transformed Europe is to survive, each of the culturally distinct units must somehow participate in the articulation of a political vocabulary that recognizes (and celebrates) others' right to be different and yet affirms the need for mutual cooperation in the pursuit of common interests and in the protection of fundamental rights.

My proposal may seem visionary right now. But even apart from the rising movements for regional identity, there are abundant reasons for ordinary people to mobilize for a federal Europe.

1. Europe can no longer rely upon the Americans and the Russians to preserve the peace. It will have to do it largely on its own. The case of Yugoslavia is only the first of many that will reveal the painful need for more decisive military peacemaking actions on the European level. Surely memories of the disastrous consequences

of nationalism in the twentieth century are fresh enough to motivate a great deal of effort to avoid the mistakes of the interwar period.

2. The emerging environmental crisis cannot be solved within state boundaries. Negotiated solutions between sovereign states give a veto to the one with the least developed environmental consciousness. This is bound to become increasingly unacceptable to many people.

3. The success of the European Economic Community in opening up national markets will place increasing pressures on each country's existing welfare programs. Those imposing heavier regulatory and fiscal burdens will find themselves at a growing competitive disadvantage in the economic struggle with less developed (and less costly) welfare states. The only solution—short of destroying the common market and returning to high tariff walls—will grant powers to the Community to establish a European welfare state that will prevent this pernicious tendency to undermine existing welfare guarantees. Granting such powers will require a reorientation of many Socialist parties, which have sometimes regarded the Community with skepticism. As they begin to appreciate the extent to which Community-wide competition endangers national welfare guarantees, they may aggressively push for the creation of a stronger political identity on the transnational level.

4. Without strong federal institutions, individuals continue to risk losing their fundamental human rights to authoritarian despotisms on more local levels. An increase in federal power on other fronts makes it more

likely that the mandates of transnational courts of human rights will serve as effective constraints on the evolution of local politics.

The prospect of war, the danger of environmental degradation, the disintegration of the national welfare state, the threat of tyranny—these dangers are already sufficiently visible that the treaties associated with Maastricht tried to deal with each of them, though in a characteristically evolutionary, and highly provisional, way.[12] The public response to Maastricht, however, makes it plain that we are reaching the limits of the elite-managed process that served the cause of European integration during the Cold War era. After a half-century of limited sovereignty, Europeans are coming to realize that they are free to control the basic conditions of their social existence—free to repeat the nationalist craziness of the past century or free to act decisively to prevent another cycle of destruction. If the Danish rejection of Maastricht serves to demonstrate the urgency of this point to liberal Europeans, it will serve the cause of the Community in the long run. Increasingly, the fate of a federal Europe will be resolved by mass politics punctuated by popular referenda, not intergovernmental deals ratified by obedient parliaments. If liberals allow nationalists a monopoly on the effort at mass mobilization, they will be digging their own grave.

Even though there will always be a constituency for xenophobia, there is presently a much broader, if diffuse, sense of a common Western European set of political values and social aspirations. The challenge is to build a political movement that will link this pan-European identity to more local cultural commitments—to allow Bavarians and Lombards and Catalans and Scots to call on their fellow Europeans to break the bonds of the nation-state and build a liberal and federal European Community.

The mobilization of a trans-Continental popular movement will, in turn, help remove the most important objection to the present efforts at European integration: the undemocratic character of existing Community institutions. As Maastricht once again shows, the leading politicians of Europe now have very little incentive to cede large powers of control to the European Parliament. To the contrary, the present situation promises them the best of all possible worlds. On the one hand, they may escape the supervision of their national parliaments by presenting these assemblies with faits accomplis that they have worked out on the Community level. On the other hand, the weakness of the European Parliament gives national prime ministers and presidents a free hand in making Community law with their associates behind closed doors.[13] There is little reason to believe that leading politicians will destroy this comfortable situation unless forced to do so by mobilized citizens insisting upon greater democracy on both the European and the regional levels. Only when faced with a serious threat of electoral retribution will national leaders consider giving up some of their authority to strong federal parliaments operating on Community and regional levels— and if they do not, a popular movement will soon supply leaders more responsive to liberal federalist imperatives.

All this assumes, of course, that ordinary Europeans are now capable of revolutionary endeavors very different from the catastrophic mobilizations that have traumatized the Continent over the past century. But if Eastern Europeans could make such an effort in the 1980s, why can't their Western counterparts take decisive action in the 1990s?

One may reply by pointing to one big difference between the two situations. The revolutions of 1989 were like many others in history—including the French, the Russian, the Chinese—in that they were provoked by the crisis of a declining empire locked in a losing competition with a more dynamic military-economic system.[14] As the weakness of the Soviet empire became visible, the question was simply whether Eastern Europeans would remain passive until the moment of Soviet vulnerability had passed and the Communist party had regrouped its forces. In contrast, Western Europe confronts another kind of crisis: nationalist grievances will begin to add up; a new generation of nationalist politicians will begin to displace an older elite accustomed to transnational cooperation under Cold War conditions; the established Community structures will slowly dissolve; and then the idea of a federal Europe will become a utopian dream. In short, the next revolution in Western Europe must be an "anticipatory" struggle by a mobilized public trying to build firm foundations for a liberal Europe before these are eroded by retrograde anxieties and nationalist demagogues. There will never be a better time to break the murderous dynamic of great-power competition that Bismarck bequeathed to his successors. But do Europeans have the insight and political capacity to undertake the anticipatory revolution that is required?

Not that a successful breakthrough will inaugurate a new era of freedom and justice for all. With free trade and free movement throughout the Community, each cultural region will increasingly contain larger numbers of outsiders, who come from other areas of Europe as part of the process of economic integration. Because regional governments will reflect dominant cultures, there will be ongoing tension between region and Community: the outsiders in each region will be constantly calling upon the European institutions to protect their fundamental right to be different. Yet this tension is likely to be less serious than in the present Europe of nations. The lines dividing outsiders and insiders will be less stark; the regions will distinguish Bavarians, Alsatians, Berliners, and Parisians, rather than Germans and French. Because there will be many more regions than nations, most regions will have very substantial numbers of natives living and working beyond their borders. Regions will be restrained in dealing with strangers, then, for oppression will generate retaliation against natives who have become strangers living in other regions.

A second problem may well become more serious instead: Will rich regions be willing to share their wealth with poorer ones? Will they successfully block redistribution schemes in the European Parliament? Will the resulting pattern of distribution be more offensive to principles of undominated equality than today's?

But we are reaching the limits of useful speculation. The question, it bears repeating, is not whether the next European revolution will be the last one in history. It is whether Western Europeans of this generation can grasp the transformative possibilities in their emerging situation and act decisively in the name—brave word—of progress.

CHAPTER FOUR

Constitutionalizing Revolution

The present revolutionary cycle in Europe may be just beginning, but it is already sufficiently advanced to require thought about the way that revolutions end.[1] Poland provides the best example. In many other areas in the East, the disintegration of Communism has not (yet) involved a full-blown revolution as I have defined the term. In contrast, Solidarity was a paradigmatic popular movement that self-consciously struggled long and hard for a new beginning in national political life. Moreover, its success in gaining power created a characteristic set of dilemmas. As we have seen, liberal revolutionaries detest the very notion of permanent revolution. They have not struggled so long merely to establish another grim period of party dictatorship.[2] But how should they use their power? Are there good and bad ways of consolidating a liberal revolution?

I shall be arguing for setting one priority above all others. Neither the privatization of the economy nor the construction of civil society should preoccupy revolutionaries first and foremost. However much liberals may want to think about such things, the organization of state power deserves immediate concern. The window of opportunity for constitutionalizing liberal revolution is open for a shorter time than is generally recognized. Unless the constitutional moment is seized to advantage, it may be missed entirely. In contrast, constructing a liberal market economy, let alone a civil society, requires decades, perhaps generations, and the project can easily be undermined without the timely adoption of an appropriate constitutional framework.

To make my case, I must work around an embarrassing intellectual vacuum. A piece of paper calling itself a constitution can be many things: an empty ideological gesture, a narrowly legalistic document, or a profound act of political self-definition. But we do not have a powerful literature describing the conditions under which constitutions of the third type come into being.[3] I try to fill this gap, at least in part, by arguing that the dynamics of revolutionary activity and the processes of constitutional promulgation may have a synergistic effect—yielding a situation in which a constitutional text can become a potent political symbol of national identity, not another bit of legalistic mumbo jumbo.*

To gain perspective, I begin by looking back to the first great age of liberal transformation: How did the American revolutionaries manage to endow their Constitution with a formative political significance, one that shaped the terms of subsequent debate and decision for generations to come? Too often, the question provokes an uncritical celebration of the unique glories of eighteenth-century America. I believe, however, that generalizable lessons can be learned from the founding—lessons that alert us to analogous challenges in the present period of revolutionary possibility. We may glimpse

*I fill the gap only in part. A constitution can also win legitimation through evolutionary processes, in which elites build consent without the support of revolutionary mass mobilizations. The most recent success along these lines has been in Spain. See Andrea Bonime-Blanc, *Spain's Transition to Democracy* (1987). A systematic comparison of recent evolutionary and revolutionary exercises in constitutionalism should be high on the agenda of future research.

important parallels between the situation confronting George Washington on the eve of the Constitutional Convention and the problem facing Lech Walesa as Solidarity took power in the aftermath of the Polish Revolution—parallels that point to the need for speedy action if Poland is to take constitutional leadership in the new revolutionary era.

Two other cases offer different perspectives. The first involves Russia, which may now be entering a constitutional moment of the kind that Poland is leaving. The second involves the establishment of the state of Israel a generation ago. A familiar pattern will begin to take shape, but this time, the window of opportunity for liberal constitutionalism slammed shut while revolutionaries busied themselves with other, seemingly more pressing matters.

Constitutional Moments

The problem of successful revolutionaries is paradoxical but real: they have won and, in winning, risk losing much of what they have fought to attain.

Not that winning was easy. In the paradigmatic case, it requires years of mobilization against the party in power—ongoing efforts to loosen the hold of the dominant political opinion and organize broad-based support for a new beginning in political and social life. Nonetheless, the existence of the old regime provided the typical movement with a common target, and having a common target served to suppress some crucial problems—notably, disagreements among the revolutionaries about important features of the political world they hoped to establish. "The enemy of my enemy is my friend"—this familiar logic made sense so long as the revolutionaries were in opposition. Why let disagreements detract from the imperative task of displacing the political regime?

With victory, the restraints imposed by the common enemy disappear. Now the revolutionaries must decide what they are for, not merely what they are against. And they must do so under circumstances in which personal ambitions are whetted by the prospect of governmental office. Leaders and followers alike find themselves more and more often in a position to appreciate how the great principles proclaimed during the period of mobilization affect their concrete interests, sometimes in surprisingly adverse ways. At the same time, new political organizations form around these concrete interests and compete for the attention and allegiance of movement supporters.

Yet in spite of these formidable diversions of political energy and attention, the members of the movement remember their struggle in the political wilderness. Can they somehow hammer out the guiding principles of their movement into an enduring form that will shape political action in the years ahead? Or will they remain passive as the political centrality of these principles is lost in the swirl of special interests seeking to gain practical advantages within the emerging state structure?

These questions define the promise of a revolutionary constitution. Writing a constitutional text offers an opportunity for a victorious movement to make a collective effort both to frame their fundamental principles and to mobilize broad popular support for their crucial initiatives. So long as these steps are taken at the propitious moment created by a successful revolution, the democratically affirmed constitutional principles may prove remarkably resistant to change even as politics becomes very unrevolutionary. Without decisive action, the liberal dimension of the revolutionary achievement may suffer great erosion, even without a massive antiliberal backlash from the general population.

I risk the appearance of antiquarianism in presenting an eighteenth-century example, especially when the constitutional moment has been grasped to liberal advantage in more recent cases. For instance, the framing and adoption of the Constitution of India has, up to now, played a positive role in sustaining a liberal democratic order.[4] Nonetheless, focusing on a paradigmatic achievement of the first great age of liberal revolution may have a special utility. Because the totalitarian revolutions of the twentieth century have gravely impaired the liberal sense of opportunity, we may perhaps repair this imbalance by glancing at 1787, when liberal revolutionaries had not yet seen their hopes shattered by the French experience, let alone by the tragic ways in which Bolsheviks, Fascists, and Nazis used the postrevolutionary moment to design horrendous modes of suppression.

The challenge is to describe the American case in terms that emphasize structural similarities to later revolutions, including those that catapulted down very different paths. First off, the Americans did not manage a peaceful revolution. On the contrary. George Washington is simply the first in a long line of guerrilla leaders who have conceded the major cities to the reactionary power while spending long years leading hit-and-run attacks from the countryside. The difference between General Washington and Marshall Giap or Chairman

Mao is that Washington refused to use his military forces for political ends after the war. Rather than playing on the many grievances of his army, Washington disbanded the troops and went home to Virginia as a civilian.

Similarly, Jefferson and Madison head a very long list of intellectuals who have established their positions by writing political tracts—what else are the Declaration of Independence and the Federalist Papers?—and by serving as civilian leaders in revolutionary zones unoccupied by the reactionary power. Jefferson and Madison differed from future totalitarians in rejecting the legitimacy of an elite vanguard party. Instead of embracing such antidemocratic models, they grasped the possibility of using constitutional lawmaking to consolidate their revolutionary principles.[5] Here I am less concerned with the substance of their Constitution than with two mechanisms they used to take advantage of their constitutional moment.

The first mechanism, the Constitutional Convention of 1787, is one of the most famous American contributions to the fund of Western political thought and practice. It involved a handful of revolutionary leaders from different parts of the country converging on Philadelphia to write a constitution four years after the peace treaty with England.

By establishing a convention apart from ordinary organs of government, the revolutionaries did more than isolate the problem of constitutional order from the many short-term issues that bulked large on the political agenda. The very creation of the separate forum created new and powerful political incentives for a successful conclusion of the experiment in constitutional formulation.

These incentives operated in a very personal way that all politicians can understand: quite simply, the revolutionary leaders risked making fools of themselves if the convention dissolved without achieving an acceptable constitutional text. Not surprisingly, this point was very clear to those with the most moral capital to lose—as any reader of the agonized correspondence between James Madison and George Washington can attest. It was absolutely crucial for Madison to persuade Washington to lend his enormous prestige to the constitutional project by chairing the convention. But why should the military hero be prepared to risk his public standing on the revolutionary intellectual's pipe dream?[6]

We should not use twenty-twenty hindsight to belittle Washington's gamble. Modern revolutionaries with moral capital of Washingtonian dimension have yet to take similar risks. Once Washington and other leaders made their decision to go to Philadelphia, however, they were engaging in a self-fulfilling prophecy.[7] They were self-consciously creating an incentive structure that maximized the chances of success by imposing new penalties for failure.

Their success should be assessed along three different dimensions. First, the revolutionaries at the convention had sacrificed much of their lives for certain fundamental principles, and a text that did not express those principles would be a failure in their eyes. Second, the delegates to the convention were perfectly aware that they lacked the resources to enact a constitution on their own authority. They could only propose a text and then campaign for its adoption by a majority of the voting population in each state. To win victory back home, delegates knew they had to protect their own region's basic interests—even when, as in the case of slavery, these interests offended the basic principles of the revolution. They could not afford the luxury of ideological purism; they would have to bargain with one another, as well as argue from first principles. Their task was to reach a sound political compromise of principles and interests through a complex process of argument and negotiation. The result hardly met with every delegate's satisfaction: one-fourth of them had quit in disgust before the convention reached agreement. Of the fifty-five who participated, only thirty-nine were willing to sign the final text, but these included many important revolutionary leaders.[8]

This suggests a third measure of success: it was not enough for a revolutionary elite to reach a constitutional solution that they considered a sound political compromise. Their final text had to be sufficiently transparent and attractive to mobilize support throughout the country. Unless their proposed constitution could serve as a popular symbol of the revolutionary generation's achievement, the posturings of a few well-established leaders would lead nowhere.

Recognizing the importance of popular support, the revolutionary leadership took a second decisive step to exploit their moment of opportunity. They appealed for support from the People over the heads of existing governments. In spite of the requirements of preexisting constitutional law, the convention refused to allow state legislatures to veto its initiative. Instead, it designed a novel procedure for bringing the popular will more directly into play.[9] Voters in each state were asked to select special delegates to ratifying conventions. These elections allowed competing candidates to concentrate on the merits of the constitutional proposal. By voting on delegates to the ratifying conventions, citizens could make a decision that was narrowly focused on the Constitution itself; they could ask themselves, Is this text an appropriate symbol of our generation's achievement? By winning these elections, the revolutionary elite could claim a special legitimacy for its constitutional text. Unlike normal legislation, the Constitution had won a "mandate from the People."

Indeed, we owe the device of the modern referendum to an analogous effort during the next great liberal revolution to exploit its own window of opportunity. Like the Americans, the French revolutionaries sought to consolidate their achievement through a constitutional text. And they are the ones who hit upon the device of the formal referendum to lend credibility to their talk of a democratic mandate from the People in support of their liberal breakthrough.[10] Of course, legal forms alone never guarantee success: the French Revolution spun out of control, with tragic consequences for the next two centuries of European history.

Walesa and Washington

The question is whether Eastern Europeans are now able and willing to pick up the thread. The news coming out of Poland is not encouraging, at least when compared to the bright prospects of 1989. At that point, the similarities with the American experience seemed striking. Lech Walesa, like Washington, was a man of courage and insight. The Solidarity movement also contained a number of powerful liberal intellectuals capable of playing Madison to Walesa's Washington. We cannot know whether the same order of success might have occurred in 1990 if the task of constitutional construction had been given the highest priority. Unfortunately, the revolutionary leadership was easily diverted. It did not sustain its sense of common enterprise long enough to elaborate a set of constitutional principles and gain the support of millions of Solidarity members and sympathizers at a national referendum. Instead, its revolutionary unity disintegrated in a blinding display of personal pettiness and intellectual hubris.[11]

Not that anyone should expect revolutionary movements like Solidarity to sustain themselves forever. It is right and proper for revolutionary leadership to split into rival parties as new problems bring new issues to the fore. It is only natural for most ordinary people to lose interest in politics as time goes on and to attend to more personal dimensions of life. Constitutional moments in the aftermath of successful revolutions represent such precious opportunities precisely because liberals reject the idea of permanent revolution. The question is whether it is too late for Poland, whether the window of opportunity has slammed shut.

Some of my Polish friends tell me that the constitutional moment has already passed; they wring their hands in the gesture of despair that Eastern Europeans have perfected over the centuries. I am not so sure. But the possibility, if it exits, will not be realized by treating constitutional formulation as one of many tasks confronting parliament. Instead, the damage that has been done may be repaired only by a gesture that emphasizes the crucial importance of seeking out a reasonable constitutional solution before the collective triumph of Solidarity becomes a bitter memory.

A special constitutional convention is urgently required—

one that includes members of Parliament and representatives of the presidency. The constitutional proposal generated by this high-visibility group should be presented to Parliament for its approval. Then, if adopted there, it should be submitted to the People for ratification in a special referendum. As we have seen, the creation of a special constitutional forum creates new incentives for the participants to reach a sound constitutional compromise.[12] But it is a mistake to evaluate the institutional innovation in terms of partisan self-interest. The call for a special constitutional forum symbolizes the present state of the revolution by asking, Is it still possible for men and women who sacrificed so much for a better Poland to transcend factionalism and clear solid constitutional ground for further democratic advance? As delegates enter the convention, they will know not only that the nation is watching them but—like it or not—that history will be judging them. Poland gave the modern world its second written constitution in 1791. Will it once again take constitutional leadership, this time with a more enduring result? By dramatizing such questions, the existence of the special forum may encourage participants to rise to the occasion and demonstrate that for all their differences, the spirit of the revolution lives on, at least in their constitutional text.

The American Constitution, it should be recalled, was not formulated in the first flush of revolutionary triumph. The Americans' first experiment in constitution writing—the Articles of Confederation of 1781—led to a pervasive political malaise comparable to the feeling in Poland today. Only after six years of dissatisfaction with this first constitutional experiment did Washington and his fellow leaders attempt a new beginning at the Philadelphia Convention of 1787. The chances for failure were as high then as they are now; but no one should underestimate the creativity of the human spirit.

Beyond Poland

The pessimists may well prove to be correct, in which case Poland's lost opportunity should go down in history as a grievous failure in revolutionary statesmanship.[13] The absence of a deeply rooted constitution will not affect Poland alone. It will also represent a tremendous loss for other nations emerging from Communist tyranny. During the 1980s, no other revolutionary movement won the widespread support gained by Solidarity.[14] Most countries are currently working with constitutional texts inherited from the Communist past, changing them in ad hoc ways to reflect new realities.[15] A constitutional breakthrough in Poland would provide an important model for weaker movements.[16]

Of these, the most crucial challenge will be confronted in the Russian Republic. The Yeltsin government is formally operating under a constitution inherited from the Brezhnev era, which has been amended more than two hundred times. The result is a legal hash and a symbolic embarrassment; surely there can be no *legitimate* order in the new Russia without a systematic effort to state the principles of the new regime. Rather than fill the vacuum with another paper constitution, the challenge is to use the process of constitutional formulation as a central vehicle for revolutionary mobilization.

This is a daunting task. The abortive Communist coup of August 1991 left behind an embryonic movement, Democratic Russia, that supports liberal political and economic development. The movement, which may embrace as many as a hundred thousand activists, provides Boris Yeltsin with an opportunity very different from that of his predecessor.[17] Whereas Mikhail Gorbachev sought to lead a revolution from above, Yeltsin can try to lead one from below—catalyzing a process through which a new constitution can become a potent symbol of the national effort at revolutionary self-definition.

First and foremost, this means that constitution writing should not be left to a small elite in Moscow, as may well occur unless decisive action is taken. The Brezhnev constitution gives formal authority to the Congress of People's Deputies—a thousand-member assembly now composed of people selected long before the popular response to the August coup destroyed the leading role of the Communist party in Russia. These old-style apparatchiks have refused to support many of the constitutional initiatives offered by the Yeltsin government. The resulting impasse can be broken in one of two ways.

On the one hand, Yeltsin may try to strike a deal with the apparatchiks: if you support my constitution, I will not call for new elections, and you can continue to enjoy the perquisites of power for your full term in office. Because most incumbents face a very uncertain electoral future, such a deal may be an effective technique for eliciting formal consent to a "Yeltsin constitution." This triumph would occur without any effort to mobilize public support for a decisive break with the past.

On the other hand, Yeltsin could use the impasse to catalyze the amorphous sentiment behind the popular victory over the August coup. Indeed, the device of a special constitutional convention seems suitable and timely. It would allow existing legislative institutions to contend with the problems of transition to a market economy. The convention itself could concurrently focus upon the political formulation of fundamental principles for the future. The elections for the convention, moreover, would provide an early occasion for Democratic Russia to generate democratic support for the new regime. For Yeltsin to be the only person in the system who has gained his office through a fair election is very unhealthy. By calling for special elections to a constitutional convention, the government could begin to detach the regime from the vagaries of Yeltsin's personality and longevity in the best possible way—by mobilizing public support for the principles of democratic constitutionalism and the rule of law.

I do not want to press my proposal too insistently. There is nothing sacrosanct about a special constitutional convention. Although such a convention is likely to take the task of constitutional formulation seriously, many plausible texts have also been produced by constituent assemblies that have exercised plenary power on normal legislative matters as well. In informal discussions, however, I have heard advocates of a plenary constituent assembly give great weight to an argument that I find unimpressive. They object to my proposal because it contemplates three democratic elections in rapid succession: one is to elect delegates to the convention; the second is to conduct a referendum on the constitution; the third is to elect legislators and a president under the new regime. "Russia cannot stand so many elections, distracted as it is by economic crisis," or so I am repeatedly told with uncompromising authority. But *when* will Russia be ready? Why will it be readier later? Two things are clear, at least to me. First, a series of elections will force the liberal groups around Yeltsin to make a strong effort to mobilize their support while the August victory is not yet forgotten. Second, a series of elections will contribute to the symbolic centrality of the constitution; elections will make it much harder for Yeltsin's successors to dismiss the Yeltsin constitution with same contempt that Yeltsin now expresses for the Brezhnev constitution.[18]

It is crucial for the formulation of the constitution to stand out in the public mind as a process involving special acts of serious consideration and popular approval. Even if the public accepts the legitimacy of the proceedings, the rule of law will be severely strained in the days of crisis that lie ahead. But without establishing the constitution on a foundation of popular consent, the task of survival will be hopeless.

Up to now, sadly enough, the Eastern European governments that have found it easiest to formulate new constitutions have been those of Bulgaria and Romania, both when under heavy Communist influence. It would be tragic if the only regimes capable of grasping the importance of constitutionalism are those dominated by former apparatchiks eager to continue their control by manipulating the symbols of liberal democracy.[19]

Is a Constitution Important?

But maybe I am exaggerating. Is it really so clear that every nation needs a Constitution-with-a-capital-C, a text that proclaims itself to be *the* fundamental law of the nation, with a higher status than all other statutes? After all, the English have been doing well enough without one for centuries. But it is one thing for a country with the liberal traditions of England to do without a constitution, quite another for nations attempting a new beginning through liberal revolution. Because these nations will characteristically find themselves with constitutions left behind by the displaced Communist regimes, the rising political elites have but two choices: to attempt a comprehensive statement of their revolutionary principles or to make do with a series of ad hoc modifications of the older Communist texts.

The second course has predictable consequences. Many authoritarian principles and practices inherited from the old regime may escape the process of ad hoc modification, even though they would have been rejected in a comprehensive revision.[20] More important, the status of constitutional norms is grievously compromised. The old Communist texts were more propaganda symbols than serious operational realities. If the aim is to transform the very character of constitutional norms, a clean break seems desirable for two different, if related, reasons.

The first involves the role that a liberal constitution can play within the structure of political identity rising from the ashes of the old regime. If constitutional formulation and ratification are given the weight they deserve, the constitution can function for the wider public as the central symbol of its revolutionary achievement and become, over time, the center of an enlightened kind of patriotism. Although America serves as an obvious example of this process, modern Germany is closer to the present scene of action. Thus far at least, "patriotic constitutionalism" has provided Germany with an under-standing of itself that can serve as a more humane and satis-fying alternative to uglier possibilities.[21] Surely the nations of Eastern Europe will require similar symbols as they strive to establish their political identity in the crises that lie ahead. When political partisans seek to exploit economic and spir-itual discontent by appealing to xenophobic nationalism, the supporters of a more open society will sorely regret the op-portunity they lost in failing to construct a constitutional sym-bol that might serve as a rallying point for a mobilized liberal politics.

My second reason for a clean break with the past concerns a narrower audience—the political elite that participates more directly in the bargaining and arguing that surrounds a con-stitutional compromise. Once these leaders sign the consti-tutional text, they will find it harder to play fast and loose with it to serve their short-run interests. Not only will they take pride in their achievement but they will have a vivid sense of the difficulty of regaining constitutional equilibrium once the original solution falls apart.

A very different situation obtains when the constitutional order emerges from ad hoc adaptation of norms inherited from the old regime. Why should either the political elite or the mass of ordinary citizens look upon brazen violations of such a text with grave concern? The question is even more pertinent when, as has been the case, ad hoc modifications are not made in a considered fashion and are not referred to the general electorate for ratification through a plebiscite.[22] The resulting softness of the constitutional norms will have different effects, depending upon the structure of authority pieced together from the institutional debris of the old regime. On the one hand, the evolving system may be bipolar, with a president and a parliament sharing control. Because the constitutional norms that putatively determine power sharing lack strong political legitimacy, the scene is set for a struggle between president and parliament that emphasizes power plays and faits accomplis. This game will generally favor the president, especially one who has gained office through popular election. As a single person, the president can act swiftly and effectively, challenging the parliament to organize its multiple membership for a suitable counteraction against those unilateral decisions.[23] As a final resort, the president can also take advantage of older authoritarian traditions and proclaim the existence of a state of emergency that justifies rule by executive decree. Whatever the outcome of this kind of unilateralism, one of the first casualties will be the idea of subjecting the conflicts between president and parliament to a rule of law that defines a stable separation of powers.

If, in contrast, a strong president does not arise in the process of ousting the Communist regime, soft constitutional norms will make it too easy for a parliamentary majority to run roughshod over fundamental rights.[24] The short history of the state of Israel provides a cautionary tale. Turn back to the late 1940s, and you will find analogies to today's situation in Eastern Europe. After decades of revolutionary struggle, the Zionist leadership could credibly claim the support of a mobilized majority of the Jewish residents of Palestine, with men like David Ben-Gurion playing a symbolic role comparable to the one played by Washington in America, Walesa in Poland, Havel in Czechoslovakia, and Yeltsin in Russia. Moreover, the authors of the Israeli Declaration of Independence grasped the significance of a rapid formulation of a constitutional text. The declaration explicitly called for elections to a constituent assembly for this precise purpose. When the assembly convened, however, it ignored its instructions. Although strong majority support for a comprehensive constitution was within his grasp, Ben-Gurion refused to make this a top priority.[25] Instead, the assembly deferred the task of constitutional formulation and transformed itself into the first Knesset, asserting plenary legislative powers in the manner of the British Parliament. Since this coup, subsequent Knessets have returned to constitution writing in fits and starts, never bringing it to completion. Forty years later, Israel has yet to promulgate a bill of rights.[26]

Meanwhile, the constitutional moment passed into history. The men and women with the greatest moral standing died, leaving others who were less confident of their ability to take constitutional leadership. The broad-based revolutionary movement fractured into a multiplicity of parties and factions. As politicians became more accomplished in serving specific constituencies, they became less interested in uniting with one another in making an overarching constitutional statement of principle.[27]

Within this second-generation setting, small parties of committed activists—in this case, religious groups of Orthodox Jews—could begin to set the ideological agenda. Although few in number, their representatives could play a strategic role in making a parliamentary majority. When other parties split apart, the ideologues could trade their support with the secular grouping that was more willing to advance their particular ideals. These tradeoffs have paid off in state support for laws that undermine liberal principles of religious toleration, enacted even though the overwhelming majority of Israelis continue to hold secular views.[28] Similar scenarios—involving xenophobic nationalist groups exploiting their parliamentary position to impose antiliberal views that are not widely held—are all too easy to generate in the Eastern Europe of the future.

Another process of erosion is no less significant. It involves responses to crises, of which Israel has had more than its fair share. In a crisis, leaders are always tempted to ignore the long-run damage to individual rights. Indeed, one statutory assault on rights often serves as a precedent for another. Although the Israeli Supreme Court has tried to check the damage, its responses would have been more aggressive if the previous generation had ratified a formal bill of rights.[29] Courts can, of course, approve emergency measures even when a bill of rights is on the books. Such concessions will lack precedential authority, however, and can be more readily reconsidered when the crisis has passed. Even in England, parliamentary majorities have proven themselves remarkably willing to limit very basic rights, including freedom of speech and freedom from arbitrary arrest.[30] The long-term costs of a short-term failure to act at the moment of revolutionary triumph are easy to underestimate.

But perhaps I have been making a more fundamental mistake. Am I wrong in suggesting that 1989 opens up a period of liberal possibilities? Surely many other currents contributed to the overthrow of Communism—religion in Poland, nationalism everywhere. Insofar as Western Europe and the United States served as models, was it their liberalism that seemed attractive or simply their wealth? Was it their promise of freedom or their advertisement of consumer paradise?

These are fair questions, to which there can be no final answers. But nothing in my argument requires me to insist that liberalism is the only, or clearly ascendant, ideological element in the current wave of transformation. To the contrary, the present fluidity itself provides additional support for my thesis. After all, if liberalism were culturally dominant, a society could look upon the constitution as a luxury—a restatement of unquestioned beliefs. In the real world, where liberalism is everywhere struggling for hearts and minds, an emphasis on constitutionalism tilts the public debate onto peculiarly favorable terrain. Although critics endlessly disdain the vulgarity and triviality of consumer society, they cannot so easily deride liberalism when the subject turns to constitutionalism and the rule of law.

Moreover, if liberals succeed in pushing the constitutional project to the center of the political stage, this initial success will give a liberal spin to the evolving pattern of debate and decision. Liberal constitutional thought and practice is far more developed than its competitors'. As a consequence, a nation breaking with its Communist past will tend to define the terms of its constitutional new beginning by considering the relevance of the American, French, Italian, and German examples to its own efforts at revolutionary renewal. Promoting constitutionalism to the top of the political agenda will thus turn the political conversation in a liberal direction. It will also tend to encourage liberal substantive decisions. In each case, only a small number of constitutional questions will prove to be politically divisive: how strong the president should be, how prominent the church should be in matters of family planning and education, and so forth. But many other dimensions of the constitution will affect the unpredictable crises and social changes that lie ahead. On these low-visibility matters of high importance, liberals will often find it surprisingly easy to use the constitution to crystallize widespread, but amorphous, commitments into legal forms that will have substantial influence upon the day after tomorrow.

I do not want to exaggerate. Like everybody else, liberals should be prepared to temper their principles and forge a constitutional compromise that will generate broad-ranging consent. To compromise requires a commitment to finding common ground. There are many Christianities, many nationalisms—some much more liberal than others. The real-world challenge is to make it hard for authoritarian demagogues to sweep away the infant constitution by successfully appealing to xenophobic nationalism or oppressive orthodoxy. To fashion a constitution that will symbolize revolutionary achievement for a variety of active groups is more important than to design a liberal utopia that will be abandoned during the first crisis.

This said, I want to resist the fashionable relativism that looks upon liberalism as a local prejudice of Anglo-American civilization or maybe even a few English-speaking universities inhabited by rootless cosmopolitans.[31] Whatever else the Eastern Europeans have been rebelling against, their experience with Communist tyranny has impressed upon them the supreme value of the rule of law and personal freedom. We do not do justice to these insights by supposing them to be foreign imports from "the West." The Eastern Europeans who have endured years of Communist tyranny are often far more alive to the importance of liberal values than the English or Americans who take them for granted. It is one thing, however, to affirm the enduring significance of freedom and the rule of law, quite another to translate these values into enduring political structures.

This is the reason I emphasize the dynamics of the process by which revolutions may—or may not—be constitutionalized. Given their protracted history of undemocratic rule, Eastern European revolutionaries desperately need to provide compelling models of a different kind of government—one in which the consent of the People is not merely a propaganda slogan but a lived reality. The effort to hammer out a sound constitutional compromise may fail: the revolutionary leadership may prove unequal to the task, or the broader population may look upon the entire exercise with cynical disbelief. Even the greatest success will be ambiguous; even the most committed will be uncertain whether they have, at long last, begun to master a legacy of arbitrary government. But the task will not be any easier if infinitely delayed. The moment to begin is when the promise of revolutionary renewal remains alive.

CHAPTER FIVE

The Mirage of Corrective Justice

Revolution and constitution—I have suggested a tight link between these two ideas. If a revolution is a collective effort to repudiate some basic aspect of the past, then a constitution offers the revolutionary polity a chance to define affirmatively the principles that will mark off the "new era" from the "old regime." Successful liberal revolutions ought to culminate in the democratic adoption of considered constitutions. Rather than naming two separate processes, *revolution* and *constitution* describe the two faces of liberal political transformation. If and when revolutionaries make the transition from negative critique to positive formulation, the constitutional text that emerges can serve as a shaping force in the evolution of political life for generations to come.

If this is right, the argument can be taken one step further by considering the extent to which a competing use of the legal system may endanger the constitutional enterprise. At first glance, this alternative legal mode seems unrelated to our inquiry. It involves the effort by the new revolutionary government to respond to demands by victims of the old regime for corrective justice. These demands can take any number of forms. Leaders and underlings of the old regime may be tried and punished for their crimes. They may be barred from high positions in the new regime. Their reputations may be destroyed by quasi-judicial findings based on old secret police files. At the same time, there may be an effort to compensate the victims: property may be returned to its "rightful" owners; substantial monetary payments may be claimed by other victims of oppression.

Because the debate on these matters is raging throughout the East, it is too early to attempt a summary of the rapidly changing patterns of decision. But it is not too early to consider basic principles, especially since they can easily be lost in stories of complicity and betrayal and forgotten in the desire for vengeance. I will emphasize the relation of this multifaceted effort to our main theme: the need to seize the opportune moment to write a constitution.[1] We must ask, To what extent does the demand for corrective justice compete with the need for effective constitutional action?

Begin by noticing the underlying similarity in the aspiration of the two legal projects. Both corrective justice and constitutional lawmaking try to draw a sharp legal line between the old order and the new regime; both seek to assure participants that something basically different has come about as a result of the successful revolutionary activity. But the two projects conceive this difference in different ways.

Three seem particularly important. The first involves the relevant time frame: corrective justice is concerned with the past and the need to punish, or compensate for, misdeeds; constitutionalism faces the future and the need to make it unlike the past. The second difference involves the legal target: corrective justice focuses on particular individuals; constitutionalism, on institutions and general principles.

These two points generate a third. If corrective justice is backward-looking and individualistic and if constitutional justice is forward-looking and systemic, both have predictable effects on the way that the revolutionary citizenry defines itself over time. An emphasis on corrective justice will divide the citizenry into two groups—evildoers and innocent victims. An emphasis on constitution writing invites citizens to put the past behind them and to think about how they all might contribute to a definition of the new order.

Constitutional creation unites; corrective justice divides. Therein lies one danger: if backward-looking faultfinding spirals out of control, the bitter divisions that ensue may divert the community from its main task, which is to prevent the recurrence of an arbitrary dictatorship by building a solid constitutional foundation for the future. After all, revolutionaries cannot rely on perpetual mass support. Their slogans—democracy, freedom, equality under law—may have gained a momentary ascendancy in the popular mind, but the commitment of most people is distinctly conditional. It is up to the new leadership to sustain consent, gaining broader and deeper support for the aims of liberal revolution.

And yet, can the revolutionary momentum continue if no steps are taken to right the wrongs of the past? Will popular support disintegrate if old-time apparatchiks not only escape punishment but emerge as leading members of the new capitalist order? This question becomes more acute as the economic transition to the market system exacts a heavy price on ordinary workers, who find that they have traded job security under communism for heavy anxieties in a market economy that lurches toward equilibrium. The severe dislocation they experience will begin to seem intolerable if old-time Communists manage to insulate themselves from market forces.

There can be no hope of abolishing the ensuing tensions; neither the divisiveness of corrective justice nor the demoralization of total amnesia can be entirely avoided.[2] But there are better and worse ways to manage the conflicts, especially given the distinctive set of political resources available to the revolutionary leadership. On the one hand, the new regime begins with an enormous fund of moral capital; unlike so many governmental leaders, the original revolutionary group does indeed have the mobilized support of millions. On the other hand, its organizational resources are limited. Depending on the revolutionary movement, the leaders may have developed a strong political organization. At best, however, this organization has not yet been stabilized and can disintegrate under stress into a multiplicity of factions. Even more significant, the revolutionary leadership cannot look upon state bureaucracies and courts with much confidence. Characteristically, these are dominated by representatives of the old regime, who can easily sabotage the implementation of new policies.

This distinctive combination—high moral capital, low bureaucratic capacity—should be kept firmly in mind as successful revolutionaries try to manage the tension between corrective justice and constitutional ordering. Responses to the past must be carefully framed in the light of predictable bureaucratic weakness. It is simple to squander moral capital in an ineffective effort to right past wrongs—creating martyrs and fostering political alienation, rather than contributing to a genuine sense of vindication. Moral capital is better spent in educating the population in the limits of the law. There can be no hope of comprehensively correcting the wrongs done over a generation or more. A few crude, bureaucratically feasible reforms will do more justice, and prove less divisive, than a quixotic quest after the mirage of corrective justice.

I develop this argument through a series of contrasts with the only case in which it does not apply: the integration of East Germany into the Federal Republic. As we shall see, the German answers to the central questions of corrective justice are problematic. But my most important point cautions against an uncritical acceptance by others of German answers. The moral-bureaucratic mix in Germany is entirely different from that prevailing elsewhere. On the one side, the West Germans have developed an impressive judicial and bureaucratic apparatus over the past forty years. Even this apparatus is being strained by the policies on corrective justice, but these strains only begin to suggest the catastrophes that will follow in radically dissimilar bureaucratic settings elsewhere. On the other hand, the governing parties in Germany do not have the same kind of moral capital as Lech Walesa or Vaclav Havel do. To the contrary: in insisting on a bureaucratically rigorous pursuit of corrective justice, the Germans hark back to their former failure to undertake a similar campaign against Nazis. However the Germans respond to their unique moral-bureaucratic situation, their response should not serve as a model for others.

The Path Not Taken

What is crucial is to minimize laborious case-by-case fault-finding—or avoid it altogether. No matter how gratifying it may be to identify evildoers and evil deeds, the systematic result will be the perpetuation of moral arbitrariness and the creation of a new generation of victims. I shall develop this theme within three different settings: the criminal trial, the novel problems posed by secret police surveillance, and the efforts by (the children of) former property-owners to reclaim "their" wrongfully seized possessions.

Begin with the classic reponse: criminal prosecution of officials, both high and low, who committed serious evil under the old regime. At present, Germany and Hungary are debating such a course, and it is beginning to emerge as a real possibility in Russia as well.[3] In each case, the prosecutors will confront problems of retroactivity: Did the wrongdoers violate laws existing at the time of their misdeeds, or were their actions so evil that Nuremberg principles apply?

This is important but familiar territory. My arguments apply even if those who consider the laws and facts conclude that criminal punishment would be justified in an ideal world. For revolutionaries are living in a very imperfect political-bureaucratic universe that is especially uncongenial to the aggressive pursuit of criminal sanctions. For obvious reasons, *liberal* revolutionaries will take the claims of criminal due process seriously. They can ill afford to begin their regime with show trials reminiscent of the Communist or Nazi past. There must be punctilious procedural safeguards: the accused must be given abundant opportunity to defend themselves with skilled lawyers; guilt must be proved beyond reasonable doubt. All this must be accomplished in a legal system that remains dominated by prosecutors and judges selected under the old regime.

This is a highly unlikely institutional setting for quick successes. Unsympathetic prosecutors may drag their heels; and even when they bring cases to court, unsympathetic judges may use the rule of law to acquit the worst evildoers. Once they take this path, the revolutionary leadership can hardly respond by creating a special system for political crimes that is superintended by "reliable" prosecutors and judges. Such a setup would stink of the totalitarian system that the revolutionaries are working to overthrow. The old judicial system is, however, only too likely to generate a series of results that will mock moralistic talk of corrective justice. Even though some of the worst evildoers may be acquitted, unsympathetic prosecutors and judges may convict some people who, if not actually innocent, seem untainted by comparison with those set free.

The potential for harm can perhaps be controlled by more precision in the use of the criminal sanction. Rather than allowing a blunderbuss prosecution of all who committed crimes under the old regime, perhaps certain categories should be singled out for attention. This seemingly sensible suggestion may prove surprisingly difficult to implement. The two obvious approaches to selective prosecution give rise to different, but related, perplexities.

Prosecutors may focus either on the misdeeds of high officials of the regime or on the wrongs of the low-level cohorts who did the dirty work of torture and murder. Prosecutions of the first type will characteristically generate hard problems of proof. High-level officials may have managed to destroy a great deal of incriminating evidence; many of their wishes were never reduced to writing in the first place. In any event, their "crimes" will generally be of the paper-pushing variety: they induced others to torture and kill but did not do the deed directly. Such circumstances always make it difficult to present a convincing case of criminal responsibility. Little wonder that the Germans, in their first prosecution of a high Eastern official, chose the minister of state security, Erich Mielke, but did not prosecute him for crimes that he committed during his long term as head of the secret police. Instead, they dredged up an ancient charge of murder made by the Nazis against Mielke in 1934. Perhaps this sixty-year-old charge is technically easier to prove, even though the eighty-four-year-old Mielke denies his presence at the scene of the crime.[4] Nonetheless, the Mielke trial has already begun to undermine the symbolic clarity of a criminal campaign against leading officials of the old regime. If the Germans succeed in inducing the Russians to hand over Erich Honecker, will they find that their documents allow them to prosecute him for nothing more serious than criminal misuse of party funds?

Focusing on low-level officials generates different problems. On the one hand, their crimes will be simpler to prove within the classic terms of the criminal law. Victims will be able to identify their torturers; witnesses may be found to corroborate scenes of degradation. On the other hand, these underlings were just pawns. I do not return here to the great point made at Nuremberg; I accept, as a matter of first principles, that the mere existence of superior orders does not exculpate the inferiors who torture or engage in other outrageous acts. My question is whether a strategy focused primarily on low-level thugs is responsive to the problem of demoralization: Will the punishment of a few underlings convince the public that the old apparatchiks are not profiting unfairly in the new regime? If the higher-ups stay free, selective prosecution of their subordinates will seem to be scapegoating; if higher-ups are prosecuted, many will avoid conviction. Is this the way the revolution wishes to spend its moral capital?

The cost of embarking on any sustained policy of criminal prosecution will be sizable. Even if the public is assured that only the worst offenders will be targeted, a criminal campaign will provoke widespread anxiety. Only a small number of heroes will contemplate with equanimity the canvass of the files by prosecutors hunting for criminal evidence. After all, who knows what will be found in the enormous amount of paper generated by the secret police and other oppressors under the old regime? Innocuous actions reported by the secret police may seem ominous when lifted from the context of everyday life in the old regime. Although convictions might be years in the future, the first steps toward criminal prosecution will have an immediately divisive effect; hundreds of thousands, perhaps millions, will fear being singled out of the general run of collaborators. Their anxiety, in turn, will affect the forward-looking project of constitutional formulation. Not only will it motivate energetic attempts, both legal and illegal, to undermine the new regime. It will also cause a crucial, if diffuse, change in the moral atmosphere: even though the risk of criminal prosecution may be objectively small, each potential target may take the threat very seriously. If millions worry that the new regime may declare them criminals, they are unlikely to identify themselves closely with the fate of the new constitutional order.

Once again, this problem does not arise with full force in Germany, where a minority of Easterners are being incorporated into an ongoing political system. In other countries, however, a policy of criminal prosecution appears in its most disadvantageous light, promising many costs but few benefits. On the one hand, these revolutionary governments lack the bureaucratic and judicial resources that allow the Germans to suppose—however unrealistically—that they can both convict the higher-ups and systematically assess the criminality of their tens of thousands of accomplices. On the other hand, if revolutionary governments are to use their window of opportunity for constitutional advantage, they must sustain the popular support that they have won in the course of their victory. Without the threat of vindictive punishment, an enormous number of minor collaborators in the old regime will be only too happy to join the liberal revolution and proclaim themselves born-again believers in freedom, equality, and the rule of law. However hypocritical these professions of virtue may seem, they will provide the revolutionary government with a new burst of popular support as it seeks to constitutionalize its revolutionary principles. Even then, the task of building firm constitutional foundations will not be easy. But is it sensible to introduce such new, and powerfully antagonistic, factors into the constitutional equation?

Although no past case is like the present ones, I fear that my argument is supported by the most important recent test of the strategy of criminal prosecution: the experience in Argentina during the 1980s. Surely the crimes committed by successive military juntas were awful by any standard—we will never know how many thousands of *desaparecidos* were killed during the Dirty War of the late 1970s and early 1980s. Few governments will be as determined to use the criminal law as President Alfonsín's Radical government was in the 1980s. Yet the attempt suffered from sobering difficulties.[5]

True, the early prosecution of nine top leaders of the military juntas was partially successful, although it incited public outrage at the acquittal of four of the nine and at the leniency of some of the sentences.[6] But it was the government's effort to move beyond the top leaders and prosecute middle-level officers that revealed the fragility that is characteristic of the moral-bureaucratic balance of insurgent regimes. Years passed as military and civilian prosecutors laboriously prepared their cases against the hundreds of majors and colonels who did the dirty work. In the meantime, the government was obliged to cope with the predictable anxiety of these officers and with their political efforts to rewrite the rules of the game.

Two years after the prosecutions began, Alfonsín was already allowing military defendants to use "due obedience to superiors" as a defense. This concession prompted a series of further retreats—amid angry street demonstrations by the left and military uprisings by the right. By the time Alfonsín left office, his government had managed to convict only a handful of wrongdoers, while a series of mitigating statutes left no more than forty military men open to prosecution.[7] This failure prepared the way for the decision by Alfonsín's successor, Menem, to pardon everybody and to release the remaining few who were still caught up in the affair.

Alfonsín's supporters in the Radical party disclaim responsibility for the debacle by pointing out that the next president was a Peronist. They ignore the facts. It was Alfonsín, not Menem, who failed to carry through the program in a systematic fashion, leaving such a bureaucratic morass that his unsympathetic successor found it easy to condemn the entire campaign. But I am not interested in apportioning blame. It is much more important to see this sad business as an example of a predictable moral-bureaucratic sequence—and one that should encourage the exploration of alternatives. Suppose that Alfonsín had not squandered his moral capital by investing so heavily in the criminal law. He could have contented himself with the speedy discharge of the worst offenders in the officer corps and taken advantage of his early popular support to call for a new constitution that placed a stringent set of institutional limitations on the military in general and on arbitrary arrest and punishment in particular. *Nunca más* (Never again)—this was the cry of the early 1980s, and what better way to assure a new beginning than to replace the often-ignored constitution from the nineteenth century with a modern text that solemnly renewed the national commitment to liberal democracy and the rule of law?

If the Alfonsín regime had compelled the military to swear allegiance to the new constitution and started to transform its promises about political and legal practice into institutional realities, would it have accomplished more in the end? Would it have been more successful in generating long-term acceptance of a constitution dedicated to gaining permanent national advantage from the tragedy of military dictatorship?

I do not know.[8] But the unsatisfactory character of the Argentine experience should lead the present generation of liberal revolutionaries in Eastern Europe to explore a different course.

The criminal law is the most explosively divisive form of corrective justice, but less traditional types of faultfinding will also seem tempting. Unless countered affirmatively, a vindictive spirit will also arise from the grave of the old regime. A primary target of all liberal revolutionaries should be the secret police. But once the security apparatus is dismantled, millions of files remain, containing reports, both true and false, about countless inhabitants. What to do with these stinking carcasses?

Burn them, I say. If the files remain, members of the new government will be tempted to use them to blackmail the opposition. This will create precedents for later abuses when ministries change hands. The resulting dynamic will be a spiral of incivility, which will poison the political atmosphere by leading to charges and countercharges, public and private, over past collaboration. The point is not whether many were guilty of this or that degree of wrongdoing. To the contrary: there were too many collaborators, and it is beyond the capacity of law and bureaucracy to assess the shades of gray accurately. Unfortunately, it is well within human capacity to use the files to blackmail political opponents for decades, leaking incriminatory material to the press whenever it seems politically convenient. Even in stable democracies like the United States, such techniques enabled J. Edgar Hoover and the Federal Bureau of Investigation to corrupt the character of political life. But their abuses will be nothing compared to the abuses that can be committed by revolutionary governments without much practice in liberal democracy.

Aside from the corrupting impact of the files on political life, there is the question of simple justice. The secret police were not content to use their own officers to spy and control the general population. They employed hundreds of thousands of "unofficial collaborators." So long as the files remain intact, politicians will be tempted to launch a bureaucratic campaign to identify all these people and impose sanctions upon them. Indeed, statutes have already been passed in Czechoslovakia, Poland, and Germany that seek to impose a variety of sanctions on collaborators, ranging from adverse publicity to a bar on further state employment.

As we shall see, a dragnet will snag on the rocks and reefs of bureaucratic procedure. But first there are matters of fundamental principle to consider. Suppose that a person named in the files as an unofficial collaborator admits that he, like countless others, was called in for questioning, but denies that he gave answers that assisted the police substantially. Suppose further that the documents say otherwise—that secret police agents assured their superiors that X was indeed a reliable collaborator. Who, then, to believe?

Even the most perfect process will make lots of mistakes, given the disorder and incompleteness of the abandoned files and the countless lies they contain. Let us optimistically suppose that the bureaucrats manage to make a mistake in only one out of twenty cases. Even so, hundreds or thousands will be falsely identified as unofficial collaborators. Is this a morally acceptable outcome? It is wrong to dismiss my question by saying that some errors are inevitably associated with all bureaucratic efforts. The new government here is blighting people's lives by giving public credibility to the most evil practices of the old regime. Should there not be an end to the power of the old secret police to destroy people's lives?

Perhaps something suggestive can be learned from American constitutional law. Time after time, the Supreme Court has been confronted by evidence seized in violation of constitutional guarantees against search and seizure. Even when

the illegally seized evidence clearly attests criminal wrongdoing, the Court has refused to allow its admission at trial.
This purist position has often been criticized. After all, the
counterargument goes, why not use the evidence to convict
guilty people and take other steps to discipline the errant
police?[9]

But this instrumental objection trivializes the principle at
stake: it is *morally wrong* for government to take advantage of
practices that violate basic principles of human dignity. The
ends, however good, do not justify the state's use of illegiti-
mate means. Whatever anyone's inclinations in this long-
standing debate, the Supreme Court's position has special
merit here.[10] We are not talking about the occasional case of
police arbitrariness. We are considering whether the new liberal regime should predictably ruin its citizens' reputations
and livelihoods on the basis of the police state's *systematic* violation of privacy and dignity. What public benefits could
possibly vindicate a course that allows the secret police to
continue injuring people?

Moreover, all unofficial collaborators are not worthy of serious condemnation. Some—how many?—did not collaborate
to receive special favors; they responded to threats against
them or their families. Should they now be publicly lumped
together with the most corrupt opportunists? And what of
those who helped the police decades ago: should the mistakes
of the distant past be allowed to ruin reputations in the here
and now? Then there is the special problem posed by people
in institutions, like the church, that maintained a limited independence from the totalitarian apparatus. These people
were inevitably involved in a double game, pacifying the au-

thorities while trying to win some protected space and gain relief for political prisoners and other victims of oppression. Even with the best process in the world, the line between excusable and inexcusable tradeoffs will be hard to draw. Once again, it is impossible to avoid the conclusion that over the run of cases, grave injustices will be done on the basis of secret police exaggerations. The new beginning will be scarred by the wrongful destruction of some, perhaps many, reputations, brought about by giving public credit to the worst evils of the old regime. Why not, then, burn the files?

And we have not even begun to consider the realities of bureaucratic administration. No Eastern country can hope to match the extraordinary bureaucratic effort presently being undertaken in Germany: 3,400 people in a Special Authority are slated to organize the chaotic mountains of materials left by the East German State Security (the Stasi). Yet for all the bureaucratic industry and the modern German tradition of due process, the early experience is full of disturbing lessons. From the outset, it proved remarkably easy for the leading media to penetrate the files and serve up a steady diet of scandalous news linking leading East German politicians to the Stasi. Now that the parliament has established a Special Authority to control the files, the new bureaucracy has managed only to change the forms of arbitrary treatment.[11]

The central problem concerns the treatment of East Germans who serve the newly unified German state as cabinet ministers or kindergarten teachers or bus drivers.[12] To keep their jobs, they must allow their employers to ask the Authority about their relation to the Stasi. The Authority does not merely supply the raw data that it has found; it provides an "expert" interpretation: "According to the files, Herr X is revealed to be an unofficial Stasi collaborator." The Authority generates such stark characterizations without hearing witnesses or inspecting any evidence outside the Stasi files. Indeed, the Authority issues its expert opinions without even guaranteeing the concerned employees a chance to read their own files and comment on the contents.[13]

In spite of this transparent breach of the most elementary notions of procedural fairness, the consequences of the Authority's expert opinions can be severe. The German Unification Treaty permits the discharge of Stasi collaborators when their continued employment by the state would be "unreasonable."[14] Given the vagueness of this standard, it is especially important to allow the accused a full opportunity to present their side of the story, so that the Authority can reach a balanced judgment about the meaning of the files: Are they the lies of overzealous Stasi agents impressing their superiors with their penetration of society? Are they the result of police coercion or enthusiastic cooperation? And so forth. Only when the Authority provides such an overall assessment can the state employer proceed responsibly to the question of "reasonable" employment and assess culpability in the light of official function. It might well be reasonable to fire a teacher for conduct that should not authorize the discharge of a bus driver.

All this is fairly obvious, as is the reason why the Authority has decided to ignore the most elementary principles of due process. If it decided to give fair hearings and reach nuanced judgments on all the available evidence, it would be completely overwhelmed by its task. The files, if neatly stacked side by side in bookcases, would extend for over one hundred miles. But the files are not neat. Many have been partially destroyed; many were never readily accessible in the first place. It will take years before the Authority's archivists gain total control over the documents. As this archival work proceeds, the Authority is trying to cope with demands for information. In the first four months of its existence, it received half a million requests for information about state employees and another half a million requests from former citizens of East Germany who wanted to inspect their own dossiers.[15] If the Authority afforded due process before it responded to state employers, its bureaucratic mill would come to a virtual halt. Of the 3,400-member staff, only fifty are expected to be fully trained lawyers. How can such a small contingent possibly handle the innumerable hearings generated by a chaotic and corrupt set of documents?[16]

Because the statute instituting the Authority does not expressly require hearings, it is perhaps understandable that the bureaucracy has not condemned itself to institutional paralysis.[17] But the result, I fear, is the systematic perpetration of injustice. Thousands of state employees have already been discharged in response to the Authority's expert opinions.[18] Worse yet, the current wave of opinions is based on a very fragmentary canvass of the files. Indeed, the Authority reserves the right to alter its expert opinions as it analyzes further evidence. A discharge on the basis of provisional opinions seems even more arbitrary. If the Constitutional Court intervenes quickly to insist upon fairer procedures, as I very much hope it will do, the damage that individuals suffer in the interim will still be severe.

Politicians are running another gauntlet: trial by newspaper. The mass media are full of expert opinions, together with snippets of supporting documentation. As one might expect, victims of character assassination are beginning to protest vociferously.[19] But Joachim Gauck, the head of the new Authority, has not responded by elaborating a sophisticated system of due process and confidentiality. He has become a leading apologist for the Stasi: "It is illogical to look upon [the files] as the product of an arbitrary fantasy. The people who popularize this view overlook the fact that the Stasi constantly worked at self-control. Sloppy work in the bureaucracy was persecuted and punished."[20]

The result is a tragically inverted drama. A high official of the Federal Republic defends the accuracy and efficiency of the Communist secret police; the accused protest their innocence; and the truth is a matter of hot dispute in the newspapers and on television. Only later do special parliamentary committees hear a fuller range of evidence from documents and live witnesses.

Where does this leave the accused politician? Thanks in part to the threatening overhang of the Stasi files, remarkably few Eastern politicians play significant roles in German politics. For example, only two Easterners presently serve as minister presidents in the five new German states carved out of the former German Democratic Republic.[21] The other three are imports from the former West Germany. Germany will have to wait for a new generation of Easterners, untainted by contact with the Stasi, before all parts of the country will contribute equally to the political process.

Although waiting will be unfortunate for Germany, it will

be catastrophic for Eastern countries that follow its example. Revolutionaries there will have to build a new political culture for themselves without the assistance of carpetbaggers from the West.[22] If they are to avoid a downward cycle of political blackmail and incivility, they should act decisively to obliterate its source.[23]

Politics aside, secret police files will have a devastating effect on many ordinary people, who will find their employment prospects and general reputation seriously damaged. At the very least, their rightful demands for *elaborate* procedural protections should be heeded.[24] But the better part of wisdom is to recognize that the search for perfect justice is beyond human capacities. Better burn the files than hire the thousands of lawyers and bureaucrats required to spin the wheels of justice in the service of an illusion.*

A bonfire will deprive millions of ordinary people of the chance to read the dirt that the secret police has accumulated about them over the decades. Some may believe that this encounter with the past might serve as a source of relief and release, a catalyst for reconciliation. This is certainly the view of Joachim Gauck, the leader of the German effort to make the files available.[25] I remain unconvinced, especially when bureaucratic realities are factored into the equation. Unless

*Some might ask, Instead of making a bonfire, why not simply seal the files for fifty years and save them for the historians? Given the success of the press in penetrating the files, I am hesitant to adopt this compromise. In my moral calculus, the risk of damaging living reputations outweighs whatever insights the future may gain in an encounter with the Stasi's version of the historical facts. One should also consider that democracy may fail to take root in one or another country, and that future dictators will then be free to use the files for their own campaigns of intimidation and persecution.

Gauck's large staff is massively increased, it will take many years to organize the files and allow most people access to them.[26] When, early in the next century, a former citizen of the German Democratic Republic learns that his suspicions about his brother-in-law were correct all along and that a report in 1969 had terrible consequences for his own career, will reconciliation necessarily follow? And how will the system respond when the beleaguered brother-in-law denies that he ever made the alleged report? Will the result of all this bureaucratic activity be the destruction of a long, if imperfect, relationship that the brother-in-law had stitched together with his relatives in the meantime?

Even if the Germans somehow manage a humane solution to these problems, their efforts should not serve as a model elsewhere. From a constitutional perspective, there is a difference in kind, not degree, between the problems of incorporating a failed Communist dictatorship into an ongoing Western democracy and the task of building a decent democratic culture from the ground up. The secret police should not be allowed to rule liberal revolutionaries from the grave. Their files do not represent a "priceless resource" enabling citizens to confront the "truth" about the past. Unless decisive action is taken, the files will poison public and private life for decades.

The German case also provides a poor guide when other countries confront the Communist regimes' mass seizure of private property. Unconcerned with the problem of creating a new constitutional order, the Germans have embarked on an ambitious program to return property to its old owners.[27] In other countries, such a program could have intolerably divisive effects, especially when homes are threatened by return to the "true" owners. The conflicts generated by such a transfer endanger the fragile sense of common purpose central to the task of constitutional construction. As with criminal prosecutions, demoralization begins long before the legal-bureaucratic system cranks out case-by-case decisions. Broad-ranging anxieties about home ownership will make people understandably skeptical about the grand free-market principles discussed in the convention hall. The construction of an enduring constitutional order is not a matter of verbal formulations and paper protections. The challenge is to write a text that will gain the deep and broad support of the general population; threatening millions of citizens with losing their homes does not seem a good place to start.

No less importantly, claims of old property owners should be viewed with caution. Although property owners were certainly wronged, they are hardly unique victims of injustice. Millions have had their lives blighted by poor education and training; large numbers have had their lives shattered by political oppression or years in prison or mental institutions. Compared to these ruined lives, property losses are of secondary importance.

It is worth emphasizing that modern liberalism does not sanctify property rights above all others. In contrast to the laissez-faire ideals of the nineteenth century, it seeks a higher goal: to enable all citizens to develop their own personality under conditions of equal freedom. Although private property and freedom of contract are fundamental aspects of this ideal, so too are liberal education and genuine equality of opportunity. Property owners have no right to demand that the

injustices they have suffered be singled out for special treatment while the more grievous injustices suffered by others
are given a lesser priority.[28]

Even within the narrow terms of property ownership, the
new order should strive for equal justice. It should resist the
efforts of owners to repossess their former buildings unless
it is prepared to give *supercompensation* to others whose property
was destroyed during the Communist regime. If we take the
logic of corrective justice seriously, owners whose buildings
were demolished by the Communists to make way for a high-
way or housing project have been injured *worse* than others:
not only were they harmed when their property was initially
taken; they were harmed a second time when it was transformed beyond recall. It is unjust to return an old building in
the center of Warsaw to one owner while inviting a neighbor
to try her luck in gaining financial compensation from some
reluctant state bureaucracy. To do so is to compound unfair-
ness in the name of correcting it.

An emphasis on repossession is also inefficient. Until property rights are clearly defined, there will be no incentive for
new investment. Given the Communist regime's neglect of
files memorializing private-property relations, it will take years
of litigation to resolve matters, and then, only rough justice
will prevail. Meanwhile, the rotting buildings of the prewar
era will continue to deteriorate, and new development will
be clogged by unending title disputes.

The early experience in East Germany is a cautionary tale.
By the spring of 1992, 1.2 million property owners had made
claims for repossession, predictably overwhelming the bureaucratic system.[29] In response to the drag on economic de-

velopment caused by clouded titles, the Federal Republic is repeatedly amending the law in an effort to escape the bureaucratic nightmare created by its earlier acceptance of the principle of repossession. Under the latest initiative, all claims must be made before the end of 1992. More significantly, remarkable procedures have been devised to allow would-be developers to curtail the possessory rights of old owners. For example, old owners have only six weeks to come up with their own plans for investment when a new investor presents a proposal for the property. If old owners fail to come up with a development proposal that is satisfactory to the special agency superintending privatization, they must content themselves with compensation, rather than repossession.[30]

It remains to be seen whether these ongoing efforts to break the economic impasse will only lead to a further bureaucratic and judicial logjam. One thing is clear: these new exceptions will do nothing to enhance the fairness of the overall system of compensation. The success of an old owner in regaining his property will now depend not only on whether the Communists razed his building to lay one of their highways but on whether a new capitalist seizes the building to execute a development plan that the old owner cannot match. If so many fail to regain their property, fairness does not require heroic bureaucratic efforts to assure other, luckier claimants of physical repossession.

What Is to Be Done?

Can nothing be done, then, to correct the grievous injustices of the past? I remain optimistic, so long as care is taken to target the worst injustices in ways that are within the weak bureaucratic capacities of the emerging regime.

I have already pointed to the most important step: the establishment of a special compensation fund. This single action will have two great advantages. The first is administrative. Establishing a special fund will allow the new government to create a bureaucracy dedicated to its administration. Because the entire bureaucratic system cannot be reformed overnight, the creation of a special task force is of the greatest importance. A group of carefully selected bureaucrats, all devoted to the new regime, can serve as a model for the new public administration. And what better goal than the speedy arrangement of compensatory payments to the worst victims of the old regime? After all, time is of the essence. If the victims are to be helped to make a new start in the new order, they should not wait for five years before the bureaucratic mills begin to grind out payments. Their claims for relief should be processed by a new breed of public official whose dedication to justice puts the old apparatchiks to shame.

The existence of a special fund will also encourage the new regime to grapple with the difficult task of setting priorities: How large should the fund be? Who should be helped first? The question, How much? is likely to prove embarrassing in revolutionary regimes with empty treasuries. There is one promising way, however, to avoid shortchanging the victims: to give them privileged access to revenues generated by the privatization of state-owned enterprises. Shouldn't the principal victims of Communism have a special stake in the funds obtained by liquidating the assets of the old regime?

This program may be especially simple to implement in those countries that follow the Czech example of distributing share ownership widely—through one or another scheme in which the general population is supplied with coupons that they may use to bid for stock ownership in companies formerly owned by the state.[31] Along with monetary payments, beneficiaries of the fund might be awarded coupons entitling them to increased shares in the new privatized firms. These coupons might go part of the way toward making the total compensation package substantial, however inadequate it may seem when measured against the hardships of totalitarian oppression.

Given harsh fiscal realities, the fund must be dispensed in ways that accord with the seriousness of relative deprivations. A rough guideline might be to allow no dispossessed property owner to get more than half as much as a political prisoner forced to spend ten years in a jail or a mental institution.[32] It is also important to make standards for compensation as objective as possible: victims should not be obliged to establish hard-to-prove facts concerning their particular treatment. If they establish that they were detained for a lengthy period without trial, or convicted for political offenses, or dispatched to a mental institution or work camp for political prisoners, that should be enough. Insofar as compensation is provided to property owners and others who have suffered lesser deprivations, standards should be framed with the realities of recordkeeping in mind. Rather than providing for full compensation for some property owners, the aim should be some compensation for all property owners.

Speed is crucial. *All* applications should be processed within two years, let us say. A target date will put the new bureaucracy on notice and encourage it to demonstrate that the new regime can *do* justice, not only talk about it.

The special fund is intended for the worst victims of injustice. A second potential remedy emphasizes the flip side of the problem: Won't apparatchiks who prospered under the old regime use their preexisting positions to gain unfair advantages in the new system?

The most fundamental safeguard here is the inauguration of a progressive taxation system. Taxing the new rich at a reasonably high rate will obligate the reformed apparatchiks to share their wealth. While this much is obvious, implementation will take a lot of work. Because the Communist regimes did not rely heavily on progressive taxation, the population is unused to making such payments, nor is there a bureaucracy in place to discharge this sensitive, and potentially oppressive, function with integrity and efficiency. The construction of such a system is a priority that is second only to the organization of rapid compensation for the victims of the old regime.

In some countries, however, the apparatchiks' success in keeping their jobs will serve as a flash point for popular resentment. Czechoslovakia provides an example. A recent "lustration" law prevents apparatchiks from holding specified state jobs for a period of five years. The Czech response, at least on paper, is draconian: not only does it deny management-level positions in all state enterprises and ministries to high members of the Communist party but it also seeks to use the secret police files to identify "conscious collaborator[s] of the State Security."[33] Because informers number in the hundreds of thousands (in a population of fifteen million), the statute will engender bureaucratic overload, individual injustice, and civil division.[34]

Interestingly, this is not the aspect of the statute that many have found troubling. Claus Offe, for example, finds fault with it for the opposite reason. The discharge of people who have served in prominent party positions, he suggests, fails to allow for case-by-case treatment and therefore offends the rule of law. Even those in leadership positions should be allowed to prove that they did nothing to merit dismissal.[35]

I disagree. Rather than immersing itself in individualized faultfinding, the sanctioning agency should take advantage of unambiguous and public facts that precisely identify the target group of *nomenklatura*. If service in a leadership position is established, we know that the apparatchik has benefited from a system that oppressed the majority. Since his past efforts at leadership led the country to economic and political catastrophe, why is it unfair to allow others to take leading positions in the new regime? Indeed, the group-oriented character of this strategy will even redound to the advantage of the discharged apparatchiks themselves. They will not suffer from the kind of stigma that typifies case-by-case faultfinding. Rather than ruining the reputations of individual officeholders, the proscription approach simply forces them to find their own way in the emerging market economy. A wholesale discharge of state officials may weaken bureaucratic functioning. But this is a question of efficiency, not justice. If ordinary workers, who enjoyed job security under Communism, must now confront the rigors and insecurities of the free market, why should

Communist bureaucrats be entitled to job security after their regime has gone bankrupt?[36]

I do not deny that wholesale discharges have significant costs, even if the enthusiasm and commitment of the replacements compensate for the loss of the superior experience of the apparatchiks. Most importantly, the discharges will create a class of enemies of the new regime, thereby running against one of the larger goals of constitutional ordering. But there is no way to completely reconcile the need to sustain popular support for the revolution and the need to avoid unnecessary divisiveness. Compared to the alternatives, a moderate use of the proscription strategy seems the best way of managing this tension.

Some will protest my pedestrian approach. Where is the passionate indignation at the crimes of the oppressors? Where is the anxious recognition of the need to expiate past sins if a society is to heal itself?

My answer recalls the partial character of liberal revolution. I do not believe that the state can save my soul—or anyone's— by a collective act of expiation, let alone a series of punitive acts against particular wrongdoers. The process by which a nation comes to terms with its own past is much more complex than the law will allow—full of ambiguities and hesitations, as well as moments of clarity and insight. It is also much more private, involving a host of mumbled confessions within families and imperfect attempts to redeem the past with future decencies. Doubtless, something is unsatisfactory about all this. But I think that we should settle for it and not suppose that the public authorities can magically transform the past by staging a series of legal rituals in which the victory of good over evil is established beyond reasonable doubt.

In warning against faultfinding, I do not want to suggest any hesitation about the legitimacy of criminal punishment. It is a necessary tool for maintaining liberal order. But I do not value pain for its own sake. There is enough pain in the world without our creating more in the hope that it will somehow ease our collective confrontation with the past—especially when the demand for retribution endangers the community-building process central to constitutional legitimation. This is the crux of the matter: if liberal revolutionaries do not act decisively to shape retributive urges into manageable forms, the revolutionary quest for a new order can all too easily degenerate into endless rounds of mutual recrimination. The challenge is to do justice to the victims of the greatest injustice without sacrificing the precious opportunity to build a strong constitutional foundation for a better future—one in which the terrors of the past will become a grim but distant memory.

CHAPTER SIX

Judges as Founders

The road I describe has not been taken. Eastern Europeans have not yet grasped the revolutionary opportunity for constitution making, and soon the moment will dissolve in the swirl of petty opportunism and narrow interests that will arise from the new power structure. But it is too soon to give up on the revolutions of 1989—and wrong to suppose they will be the last in world history.

Given present uncertainties, however, alternative paths to liberal constitutionalism should be considered. If revolutionary politicians don't try to build strong support for the constitution among the People, can anybody else undertake the task? The most likely candidate is the judiciary. Throughout Eastern Europe, courts have begun to intervene on a host of politically sensitive issues. This process has advanced most rapidly in Hungary, whose constitutional court has handed down a remarkable series of judgments on everything from abortion to capital punishment to the redistribution of property to the prosecution of wrongdoers under the previous regime.[1] But judges are claiming newfound powers in many other countries, including Russia.[2]

American judicial practice may seem to inspire this activity. The analogy is frequently invoked, but I have already suggested reasons for caution. John Marshall was not operating in a political vacuum when he started carving out a new constitutional role for courts in his epochal decision in *Marbury v.*

Madison. He could never have succeeded without the earlier political triumphs achieved by Washington and his fellow leaders at the Constitutional Convention. It was they, not Marshall, who mobilized the American people in support of the Constitution. To be sure, Marshall brilliantly used this political triumph to catapult the Court into a special position as defender of the Constitution. But he could not have created this role on his own, as some of the Eastern European courts seem to imagine.

Moreover, Marshall's fame should not conceal the extreme caution with which the early Supreme Court invoked its powers over congressional legislation. *Marbury*, decided in 1803, was the only decision in Marshall's long tenure as chief justice that invalidated an act of Congress—and it involved a minor jurisdictional provision that affected no powerful political interest directly. Not until 1857 did the Court screw itself up to declare another congressional statute unconstitutional.[3] Only eighty years after the founding—in the wake of the Civil War—did the Supreme Court gradually become more assertive.

The American example of judicial review has undoubtedly inspired judges elsewhere. But its slow and painful development in its native land does not encourage hopes for a quick transplant, especially in such uncongenial soil as Eastern Europe. Communism gravely weakened the uncertain tradition of judicial independence that Eastern Europe had inherited from the Austro-Hungarian and Russian empires. The jurisprudential context in which Continental courts operate is also radically different from that of their American counterparts. American judges live within a larger common law tradition that places a high value on judicial creativity and recognizes case law as an important source of legal doctrine. The tendency in Europe, however, is to deny emphatically the legitimacy of judicial creativity. At the same time, the high prestige of the judiciary in America contrasts painfully with the low estate of the judges of Eastern Europe. To put the point gently, being a judge was not a high-status occupation under Communism. Most first-rate people went into less politicized professions, like science and engineering. Even within the law, the public prosecutor often had more prestige than the humble judge. Given the low status of the judiciary, why should the new generation of politicians and police follow legalistic edicts when doing so proves inconvenient?

If the only example of successful constitutional review came from the United States, I would view the present burst of Eastern European activism with the greatest skepticism. Do not be overly impressed by the early successes of these courts in gaining politicians' acceptance of their rulings. After the first flush of revolutionary enthusiasm for the rule of law fades, so too will judicial authority. Even after two centuries, American courts struggle—often in vain—against political resistance. The John Marshalls of Eastern Europe will be swept away at the first severe crisis.

A More Helpful Precedent?

But the American example does not provide the only benchmark. For all its differences, the German case seems more relevant—and more hopeful—than anything from across the Atlantic. Like Eastern Europe today, post-Nazi Germany tried to break with its totalitarian past, yet many of its judges were deeply compromised by their participation in the old regime.[4] German legal culture also exemplified the jurisprudential mentality now prevailing in Eastern Europe—indeed, Germany has served as a legal source for many codes and doctrines in these countries. Yet, like Eastern Europeans today, Germans lacked a strong tradition of constitutional review. However proud they may have been of their legal science, they had focused on the classic problems of civil and criminal law; their leading studies of constitutional law did not place courts at the center of their concern. This emphasis reflects the very problematic status of judicial review under the Weimar Constitution.[5]

Against this background, the Constitutional Court's great success in the postwar years deserves respectful attention in Eastern Europe. Not only did the Court exercise its authority early and often but it has been remarkably successful in winning legitimacy both from political elites and from the general population. Its substantive decisions sometimes show a greater appreciation for liberal values than American courts have managed to achieve after two hundred years.[6]

The suggestiveness of the German experience is heightened if we overcome the limits of hindsight. When sixty-five West German politicians met in 1948 in a special parliamentary council to frame a constitution, they had no way of anticipating the economic boom of the 1950s and 1960s.[7] All they saw around them was the ruin and misery of war. Looking past this wreckage, they confronted a history of failure—the failure of the Frankfurter Assembly to constitutionalize the liberal revolution of 1848, the failure of the Weimar Assembly to construct an enduring constitution in 1919, the failure of the German People to repudiate Nazism on their own, despite the crazy decision of their wartime leaders to fight on long after victory was impossible. Worse yet, the council represented only a segment of the German People—those who had escaped Soviet occupation—and it met only at the sufferance of the Western Allies.

As in the case of Eastern Europe, the Basic Law was originally promulgated without a full-fledged mandate from the German People. This was no accident. Traumatized by Nazism as they were, the early leaders were painfully distrustful of the German population. Their mistrust was reflected not only in public statements but in the way that they went about getting the new Basic Law ratified.[8] The founders of the Federal Republic refused to submit their constitutional proposals to the People in a referendum. Ignoring the explicit expectations of the Allied powers, the founders refused to demonstrate that their proposed Basic Law could win the mobilized support of a strong majority of German citizens.[9] They contented themselves with a less demanding ratification procedure, which required two-thirds of the West German state legislatures to give their approval.[10] To emphasize the provisionality of their initiative, the founders refused to call their text a constitution, instead using the novel circumlocution Basic Law.[11] Indeed, their Basic Law closes with a provision for its replacement with a *real* Constitution later on—most notably, through a constitutional convention that might include representatives from East Germany as well as West Germany. Still, these "soft" norms are the bricks of the enduring structure that the Constitutional Court has managed to build.*

Three Structural Principles

What was it about the constitutional position of the Constitutional Court that allowed it to attempt this generation-long task? Three points stand out, involving structure, jurisdiction, and independence.

Although the structure of the German court may seem odd to Americans, it will not cause much trouble if adopted in Eastern Europe. In the United States, the Supreme Court sits at the top of the judicial system and can review all issues of federal law, including the meaning of statutes. The German Constitutional Court focuses exclusively on the meaning of the Basic Law. Specialization has two advantages—one legal, the other political.[12] Legally, it frees judges from the reigning dogmatism of the civil law tradition and allows them to reflect self-consciously on liberal values in the course of adjudication. Politically, it encourages the selection of judges who are un-

---

*My talk of softness should not obscure an important difference between the German case and the typical situation in Eastern Europe. The German assembly that proposed the Basic Law resembled the American Constitutional Convention in that it was a special-purpose body that concentrated its energies on the single task of constitutional formulation. In contrast, no Eastern country has yet made such a focused effort at designing a comprehensive framework. Perhaps softness comes in at least two degrees. The German Basic Law has one degree: its failure to gain popular ratification. Many of the Eastern countries exhibit two degrees: they have not promulgated a new and comprehensive constitutional proposal, much less exposed it to the rigors of popular referenda.

tainted by close association with the old regime. The German Court owed much of its early legitimacy to the fact that, in contrast to the other courts, former Nazis were not allowed to join the bench.

It follows that an appropriate mechanism for the selection of judges is a matter of high constitutional importance. Once again, America serves as an anti-model. Because justices hold office for life, and because there are only nine of them, every nomination becomes a matter for fierce political contestation. Recent battles like those over Robert Bork and Clarence Thomas would not enhance the legitimacy of an infant institution. The German system lowers the stakes involved in any single nomination, allowing selection to proceed without hyperpoliticization. German justices serve only for twelve years, without possibility of renewal. Limiting the term allows a second innovation: the scheduled vacancies do not expire one at a time; two or more seats are filled during the same session of parliament. Political parties need not regard judicial nominations as if "the winner took all" in the American manner. Given several open seats, it makes more political sense for the two main parties to share the seats between them, regardless of who is in control of the government.[13]

This result is foreordained by the special voting rule governing the process: nominees must gain two-thirds support in one house of parliament. Neither major party has ever won such a supermajority, so each can veto the nominations of the other—thus making a decision to divvy up the positions the only sensible solution. Not that the parties feel themselves free to fill "their" slots with extreme partisans: the possibility that their opponents may veto provocative appointments encourages the selection of men and women with reputations for moderation and judiciousness. And it is precisely this kind of reputation that an infant court will require if it hopes to sustain itself in constitutional struggles with the other branches of government.[14] The German arrangement has nothing sacred about it; other Western European constitutions contain rather different variations on a common theme. What is key is the way in which voting rules and the bundling of appointments interact, not just to discourage the major parties from making the selection of judges into a game of political football, but to encourage them instead to place men and women of repute, integrity, and moderation on the Court.

This mechanism seems superior to the winner-take-all American system. It is also preferable to an alternative that has deeper roots in Continental traditions. European judges are civil servants, beginning their careers shortly after graduation from law school. Given the existence of a corps of professional judges, constitutions have sometimes allowed judges a say in naming at least some of the members of the constitutional court. Although this model has recently been followed in Eastern Europe, it seems a serious mistake in a postrevolutionary setting.[15] The professional judges owe their appointments to the old regime; to transform Communist hacks into guardians of the new order is wrongheaded.

But we have only begun to explore the secret of the German court's success. A great deal of its legitimacy is linked to the fact that ordinary individuals can gain immediate access to it. Elsewhere, constitutional courts have often been granted a narrower jurisdiction; problems are referred to them by members of parliament or judges of the civil courts or other high officials of government.[16] A broad jurisdiction allows the court to generate its own symbolic linkages to the ordinary citizen. For millions who will never get to the court, potential access symbolizes the seriousness of the new regime's commitment to limited government and individual freedom.

There is much more than a symbol at stake. By opening wide the doors of the court, the constitution puts the judges in a better position to establish an appropriate form of independence from ordinary politics and destructive power plays. Consider the dilemmas confronting a constitutional court whose jurisdiction is limited to complaints raised by a small group of government officials, such as a parliamentary faction or constitutional organs of the government. When dealing with such politicized situations, the infant court has two options: it can declare the controversial statute constitutional and run the risk of seeming to be a rubber stamp, or it can invalidate the law and find itself embroiled in a high-profile struggle with the parliamentary majority.

Now consider how the introduction of broader jurisdiction ameliorates this dilemma. Rather than confining their attention to a few political hot potatoes tossed to them by government officials, the judges will be deciding cases from ordinary life at its most diverse. Most cases will not involve matters of pressing importance to politicians sitting in the nation's capital. They may involve instead the plight of an ordinary man or woman arbitrarily arrested by the police, or the casual suppression of speech by a local potentate. By intervening decisively in such cases, the infant court will not be obliged to vindicate the constitution at the cost of provoking intense parliamentary opposition. Its decisions may crystallize a consensus on fundamental principles and rights, rather than precipitating harsh political counterattacks. For a constitutional court entirely to avoid political controversy is both impossible and undesirable. Nonetheless, the German Court has been greatly advantaged by the sorts of items on its docket—which mostly consist of complaints by ordinary citizens, rather than the abstract and politicized grievances of government officials.[17]

I would go one step further and suggest that the new revolutionary regimes reject the German idea of controlling abstract norms completely. In this connection, the American model has something to offer. From the beginning of the republic, the Supreme Court has refused to offer advisory opinions on the abstract constitutionality of statutes, waiting instead for a concrete complaint before it renders judgment.[18] Some of the reasons for this reticence have no resonance in Europe, for they express the particularistic biases of an Anglo-American tradition far removed from the spirit of Continental legal thought.

But reasons for caution remain. Quite simply, if a court must wait for a specific complaint by an ordinary individual, it may take a while before a bitterly politicized dispute makes its way into the judges' chambers. This delay provides the court with a valuable political resource in its struggle to sustain itself as part of the new constitutional order. After a year or two, a hotly contested initiative may have lost some of its sting. A judicial decision that could have propelled the court into a losing battle with an outraged parliamentary majority might, two years later, be received in a more measured way. The pause may also permit the court to make a better decision—giving it a perspective easily abandoned in the heat of a partisan contest.

These points have often been emphasized by American scholars trying to account for the Supreme Court's success in sustaining its constitutional legitimacy.[19] They would bear repeating right now by Eastern European jurists. In a report on the first year of Hungary's constitutional court, Chief Justice Laszlo Solyom emphatically rejects a focus on concrete cases, dedicating his Court instead to the more abstract issues raised in petitions by presidents and legislatures: "A constitutional court when limited to the abstract norm control, does not have any cause to hold trials. We do not need to clarify any facts through the debate of opposing parties; the legal arguments of the petitioner ... are in fact indifferent, since we can listen to experts and the friends of the Court. All this can more easily be arranged in writing; but it is our business as to what sort of help we intend to use to form our opinions."[20] Given this lofty conception of the court as a free-floating problem-solver,[21] Solyom does not find it troubling that "the Constitutional procedure [has developed] into some 'secret' activity behind closed doors." In his view, the turn to secrecy is merely a consequence of a justified refusal to "undertake the burdens of formal publicity" and the court's desire to make "decision proposals right away."[22] If the American Supreme Court had adopted anything resembling Solyom's secretive and assertive stance, it would not have survived a single generation of its turbulent history. Does the Hungarian Constitutional Court suppose that it operates under more favorable conditions?

My anxiety is all the greater when I look at the substance of the Court's early decisions. As a whole, these strike me as admirable. The Court has pushed Hungarian law in the right direction in two fundamental areas considered in preceding chapters. On the one hand, it has invalidated legislative efforts to repeal the statute of limitations so as to allow the wide-ranging criminal prosecution of Communists. On the other hand, it has forced the legislature to consider a variety of inequities involved in allowing some people to reclaim their property while denying others this remedy.[23] But the Court cannot expect to play this positive role over the long run without displaying much more political prudence. The intrinsic merit of its legal positions is hardly a guarantee of continuing political viability—especially in the case of a soft constitution like Hungary's, which has never been subjected to a wide-ranging and intense public debate in a special referendum.[24] It is only a matter of time before the Court's abstract resolution of an unending series of burning disputes will generate an overwhelming reaction by parliamentarians, who will try to destroy such a politically exposed institution.[25]

This grim prospect leads us to consider a final crucial variable: the extent to which parliament can overrule the court by amending the constitution. Germany's Basic Law imposes a distinctive two-part system on the process of revision. If two-thirds of the members of parliament do not like what the Court has done on most matters, they are perfectly free to amend the Constitution. In contrast, parliament is completely disabled from amending certain constitutional guarantees—most notably, those protected by the foundational commitment to human dignity proclaimed by the First Article of the Basic Law. The Constitutional Court thus has an exceptional degree of institutional autonomy in defining basic human rights, which allows it to stand its ground against authoritarian outbursts that would overwhelm more vulnerable institutions.[26]

Perhaps this kind of absolute entrenchment permits the judges too much leeway for irresponsible decisions.[27] Nonetheless, I think that robust constitutional insulation is important. Not only will it protect the emerging order during the brief but acute periods of crisis that are an inevitable part of political life. The very existence of an ultimate safeguard will also increase judicial self-confidence at all times during the first generation or two of development.

Yet constitutional insulation, or anything resembling it, seems unlikely in Eastern Europe so long as it continues to settle for constitutions produced by piecemeal changes of Communist texts. Although the German founders refused to submit their Basic Law to the test of a plebiscite, at least they convened a special constitutional assembly, independent of any parliament, to write a text that comprehensively sought to avoid the horrors of the totalitarian past. Within this institutional context, it seemed plausible to make a special effort to protect fundamental rights against destruction even by a parliamentary majority. In contrast, the chances for such strong insulation are reduced when the task of constitutional formulation is given to an ordinary parliament. It would take a very remarkable group of deputies to recognize that they themselves might find it politically expedient to destroy rights—and then take decisive steps to make it especially difficult for future parliaments to take such destructive actions.[28]

Nonetheless, if a parliamentary opportunity arises, reform should have an overriding aim: an amendment procedure that

makes it impossible for a single session of parliament to mod-
ify provisions defining fundamental human rights. Requiring
the approval of at least two parliaments will give the court
much greater capacity to withstand the immediate shocks that
are a predictable part of the ongoing effort to protect human
freedom against repression.

Even assuming that an enlightened parliament might enact
such a self-limitation, the German model of constitutional development still remains second-best. A revolutionary liberal
movement should not depend on the benign decisions of a
political and judicial elite to define and guarantee its basic
rights. Perhaps Germans could expect no better at a time of
Allied occupation and Nazi catastrophe. But unlike the Germans, the Eastern Europeans come to the task of constitutional construction with one great advantage: to one degree
or another, *they are liberating themselves from Communism*. The challenge is to channel the political energies released by this movement and seize the moment to mobilize popular support for
a liberal constitution.

Once this affirmation of political identity has been made,
the judges can far more easily, and appropriately, insist on
their authority to take the text seriously. No longer will they
be teasing out fundamental commitments from ad hoc revi-
sions of the old order.[29] They may stand their ground on the
constitutional principles affirmed by the People in a national
referendum and stipulate that unless these principles are
amended, they should bind even the most powerful officials
as rules of law.[30]

CHAPTER SEVEN

The Meaning of 1989

It is one thing to sit on the sidelines and point emphatically to the window of opportunity closing upon the revolutions of Eastern Europe, quite another to act decisively and gain democratic consent to a constitution that defines the terms of political life for a new era. It would be wrong, moreover, to exaggerate the significance of my constitutional concerns. Even if my fears are realized, it would hardly be the first time in world history that a rising political movement has failed to exploit its opportunities to the fullest. It will be more than satisfactory if most Eastern Europeans—through leadership, luck, and popular support—manage to muddle their way toward liberal democracy, avoiding the worst excesses of xenophobic nationalism that might serve as a cover for new authoritarianisms.

If this much can be accomplished, the revolutions of 1989 will have enduring importance for all of us, however removed we may be from the scene of the action. By exploiting a moment of Communist weakness, the Eastern Europeans have not only destroyed a great system of oppression but given us reason to rethink the promise of revolution itself. In spite of the tragic consequences of revolutionary mobilizations since 1917, the century closes with a great affirmation: men and women can make a new beginning and build a better world—one that won't look anything like utopia but that still promises more diversity and freedom than the grim bureaucratic tyranny it has replaced.

What are the rest of us to make of this triumph, if such it turns out to be? I have already emphasized the importance of this question for Western Europe. After briefly returning to this point, I shall consider people, like myself, who stand on the sidelines in Africa or the Americas or the rest of the world. Because liberals in these places confront very different problems, the Eastern European success carries very different meanings—but do these meanings suggest the continuing relevance of the revolutionary project?

As we have seen, the central challenge for liberals in Western Europe does not involve the construction of a rights-oriented market economy. It is posed by the danger that a resurgent nationalism will wreck efforts at European federation begun by political and economic elites during the Cold War. Nonetheless, the example of the Eastern European revolutions may provide important resources in the coming struggle against the Western European state system. The Easterners' success in mobilizing themselves for constructive political change may soften the brittle fears of revolution generated by the terrors of the twentieth century. If these Easterners can redefine the basic terms of their political existence, why not Westerners as well?

The answer given in the West will, in turn, have a powerful impact on the East. If Westerners mobilize and give deeper political meaning to the European Community, this revolutionary dynamic will reinforce those in the East who are working for liberal constitutional solutions; if Westerners relapse into a retrograde nationalism, the impact in the East will be devastating. At the same time, the fate of the constitution-building project in the East will rebound onto the West. If liberal democracy fails in the East, the West will find itself reeling under the pressure of millions of asylum seekers trying to escape a new round of authoritarianism and impoverishment; mass migrations, in turn, could inflame nationalist sentiment and tip the balance in the Western struggle between liberal federalism and retrograde nationalism.

Both in the East and in the West, the Europeans' success or failure to capitalize on the revolutionary possibilities opened up in 1989 will shape the destiny of the entire planet for a very long time to come. This is the reason why I have added an American voice to the ongoing European debate. Neither the Atlantic nor the Pacific are big enough to insulate the rest of us from Europe's blunders and triumphs. We are all interested parties.

As the struggle over European identity proceeds apace, 1989 will also have an immediate, if subtler, impact on others' efforts to define their own political predicaments. Can we begin to glimpse how the reemergence of liberal revolution is reshaping the terms of political definition in the rest of the world?

Beyond Europe

My essay began by rejecting the idea of total revolution. This is a notion that can admit only of a theological interpretation, as when Christ entered history and, in the eyes of believers, radically transformed the very nature of Being in the World. Liberal revolutionaries reject such totalizing transformations. They deny that mere mortals can coherently attempt radical escapes from history. Every new beginning is partial, carrying along with it much of the cultural and practical baggage of the past.

The revolutionary project is not therefore pointless; people aren't gods, but they aren't brutes either. Although they cannot escape history, they are not fated to repeat endlessly the habitual patterns of the past. The fundamental, if partial, critique and reorganization of social life will continue to distinguish human beings and provide them with a significant degree of control over the conditions of their existence.

Perhaps this is not saying much, but it is about all I can muster when asked to state the general significance of the reemergence of liberal revolution as a world-historical possibility. Because liberal revolutions are always partial and depend on the local background of received practices and ideals, the meat of the discussion will always be found in the details, which I cannot provide here. Nonetheless, a few glimpses around the world may serve to orient future inquiry.

At present, the most revolutionary situation is in South Africa, which confronts challenges very different from Europe's. There is little danger that the constitutional moment will go underappreciated. To the contrary: negotiation over a new constitution provides the crucial mechanism through which politically mobilized blacks and whites will try to work out the terms of their new beginning together.

Both Mandela and de Klerk have been remarkably skillful in channeling the hopes and fears of their constituents in liberal directions. The question is whether this effort at constitution building will continue or whether it will disintegrate into mass violence and blind acts of retribution for past wrongs. Within this context, the image of Eastern Europe plays a modest, but helpful, role. Most important, it will soften the hard-line Marxist element in the African Nationalist Congress. The collapse of Communism in Europe provides a chance to retreat gracefully from the tired Marxist doctrines that have impoverished so much of Africa. With Communism so obviously on the retreat worldwide, hard-liners cannot easily pretend that a bright socialist future awaits South Africa at the end of history. Perhaps the working class should instead push aggressively for its interests within the constitutional framework of a rights-protecting, market-oriented, private property system?

Black acceptance of a liberal political economy will be an incentive for whites to continue their present course of interracial accommodation. De Klerk has brilliantly mobilized his own constituency at a crucial referendum in support of constitutional compromise. After gaining a decisive victory at the polls, he is now in a strong position to respond affirmatively if Mandela can credibly commit his movement to a liberal democratic constitutional solution. Even if the liberal center holds, both sides will still have plenty of extremists to deal with. But think how much harder the task would have been if the worldwide Communist revolution had continued to inspire ANC activists and to haunt the future for so many whites.

For all its importance, South Africa is a variation on an old theme: a revolutionary movement challenges an entrenched European structure, using the symbols of nationalism and socialism to mobilize the colonial population against oppression. As we look around the world, it is hard to identify many other places in which this story is likely to repeat itself: Peru? Cambodia? the Philippines?

In contrast, a new scenario is recurring with increasing frequency and importance. I will call it the "second-generation" dynamic. It involves nations that have successfully engaged in colonial revolutions during the past century. Some of these revolutions were straightforward applications of the Bolshevik model. But many had much deeper roots in local culture; the revolutions in places as different as Mexico and India, Israel and Algeria, were all mass mobilizations originally inspired by a mix of socialist and nationalist ideas. Many other movements failed to generate the same level of active popular support but were nevertheless culturally distinctive— Baathist Socialism in the Middle East, for example, as well as many African socialist movements during the first generation of independence.

All these revolutionary enterprises confront a similar problem. The generation that won the earlier victories is dead or dying; the old proud nationalist and socialist slogans now serve as a cover for a corrupt bureaucracy. The challenge for a new generation is to renew and redefine a political direction. In this context, the European revolutions of 1989 have a shattering symbolic impact. Here is the emerging scenario: the European revolutions, together with the local failure of central planning, encourage political elites to recognize the need for fundamental change. To win a liberal breakthrough, however, will not only require the sensitive implementation of market-oriented, rights-protecting, liberal programs of economic and social development. Reformers must also gain widespread popular support if they hope to defeat the entrenched bureaucratic and economic interests that were built up in the previous round of revolutionary development.

The most promising experiments in such liberal transformations have been in Latin America. Both Mexico and Argentina provide variations on a typical situation: leaders emerge to head political movements—the PRI in Mexico, the Peronistas in Argentina—that had previously won revolutionary triumphs on the basis of nationalist and socialist goals. Nonetheless, both Salinas in Mexico and Menem in Argentina are attempting broad-ranging liberal reforms that increasingly challenge their inherited symbols. Will they be able to mobilize a large section of their traditional working-class constituency, together with the middle classes, to support a decisive liberal breakthrough? Even if such "revolutions from above" fail, will insurgent leaders emerge to attempt liberal revolutions from below, as in Poland and Russia?

At the moment, the United States occupies one of the few zones untouched by the threat or promise of liberal revolution. Americans may welcome the new possibilities opened by world transformation but seem curiously untouched—as if they were unmoved movers or self-satisfied voyeurs?

Since the Enlightenment, America has served as the leading exemplar of liberal revolution. James Madison, Abraham Lincoln, Martin Luther King, Jr.—these people and many others gained political leadership at the head of citizen movements for self-conscious change. After a generation of sacrifice and debate, the movements won the mobilized assent of a majority of Americans to a new beginning in their relationships with one another. Many of these collective acts of renewal have pushed the polity in a liberal direction—toward the separation of church and state, toward the protection of free markets, and beyond formal equality toward social justice.

I am the last to deny how far America falls short. Along many dimensions, it fails to assure a level of social justice taken for granted in European social democracies. Nonetheless, the American success in mobilizing citizen energies for constructive change during both the New Deal and the civil rights eras played an important role in the twentieth-century struggle against Fascism and Bolshevism. While traumatized European liberals like Hayek were proclaiming that the pursuit of social justice was paving the road to serfdom, American liberals could remain more skeptical about apocalyptic antirevolutionary appeals. Whatever their substantive limitations, the New Deal and the civil rights movement gave tangible demonstrations of a different possibility: that men and women might work together to make new beginnings in their collective pursuit of a more just and free society.

How, then, to greet the great news from Europe? It could—should—be a reminder of the American past and a challenge to take up the burden in our own time. Surely, hoping for success any time soon would be foolish. Americans are living in a period of "politics as usual." At no time since the 1920s have the established political parties generated so little interest among ordinary Americans. But at least two movements beyond the parties have real thrust: environmentalism and feminism have mobilized broad publics and elicited sustaining political interest. Neither of these movements, however, has put its first priority on joining forces with more established civil rights and labor groups to deal with the single most pressing crisis: the disgrace of the American ghetto. Without an enormous effort to educate the next generation of ghetto kids, Americans will be confronting a pathological level of alienation from the civic enterprise early in the next century. A civilized liberal democracy will not survive if Americans allow their major cities to become centers of a proliferating underclass without education or hope.

We did not need the Los Angeles riots to make this obvious. The question is whether Americans have the political will to do something serious about it. Liberal revolutions are hard work, requiring millions to set aside their private interests to concentrate on the task of political renewal. In each generation, there have always been some Americans willing to make this sacrifice. But can they mobilize the majority of their fellow citizens in support of social justice? Americans will be in real trouble if they remain on the sidelines much longer, leaving it to others to carry the torch of liberal revolution into the new century.

The End of History

The defeat of Communism hardly represents the end of history. It is best likened to the end of a civil war between two children of the European Enlightenment. Despite their struggle, both communists and liberals agreed on many things: the separation of church and state; the repudiation of traditional caste, gender, and racial hierarchies; the rejection of xenophobic nationalism; and the pursuit of social justice. The battle raged onward because the combatants rallied behind very different versions of these Enlightenment ideals; when taken together, all their differences added up to a radically different understanding of the nature of state authority and the character of human freedom.

The end of the civil war, however, has left the winning side in a traumatized condition. No longer can it fight a negative battle against the transparent evils of bureaucratic totalitarianism. It must engage in a positive struggle to realize its own ideals of freedom and equality, and it must build a political order that will inspire dedicated support from a diverse and critical citizenry.

This must be accomplished in the face of resistance by formidable opponents. Religious fundamentalists in much of the world reject liberalism's separation of church and state, its insistence upon each person's fundamental right to define his or her own heaven and hell. Neo-Confucian societies in Asia resist liberalism's challenge to traditional hierarchies, its celebration of the right to be different. Indigenous cultures in Africa and parts of Latin America may find Enlightenment values even more difficult to appreciate.

Given this world setting, it is a thousand years too soon to suggest, with Francis Fukuyama, that victory in the civil war with Communism leaves liberals no choice but to return to the paltry consumerist satisfactions of market society.[1] The truth is very different: if we seize the moment, if we expand the range of functioning constitutional democracy beyond the liberal heartland, perhaps we can provide convincing evidence that liberalism *deserved* to win the struggle in 1989. In history at least, nothing succeeds like success. Liberals in Germany succeeded in constructing a functioning democracy in the aftermath of Nazism—an achievement that, as we have seen, today serves as a model for further acts of constitutional construction. If liberals succeed today in Poland or Russia or South Africa, their triumphs will suggest to others that liberal revolution is not a hollow hope but a live political possibility.

Further successes may, in turn, inspire others in the more remote future to look back upon 1989 as a historical watershed. It was then, they may say, that the promise of the French Revolution finally began to be redeemed after the horrible false starts and shattered hopes of the twentieth century. Perhaps they will even indulge in the luxury of explaining to their children why the triumph of liberalism was historically inevitable.

But we know otherwise. As likely as not, the world of 2020 will have a very different appearance. It will contain a Europe of hostile nation-states and an America impoverished by economic nationalism, racked by ethnic division and the alienation of hopeless slums. This self-proclaimed First World will look out upon a larger complex of competing xenophobias and bitter proletariats while it gasps for breath in an environment that all have mindlessly conspired to destroy.

The promise of 1989 will have vanished like a dream, and this book will serve as a bitter reminder of liberal illusion.

Notes

1
A New Era

1. Hannah Arendt, *On Revolution* (1963). For an intelligent critique of approaches by contemporary social scientists, see S. N. Eisenstadt, *Revolution and the Transformation of Societies* (1978). See also the useful bibliography supplied in John Dunn, *Modern Revolutions: An Introduction to the Analysis of a Political Phenomenon* 295–339 (2d ed. 1989).

2
Rethinking Revolution

1. It is very common for revolutionaries to divide time into further segments. For example, many have looked back to the day before yesterday and found a golden age that preceded a more recent period of catastrophic decline. This three-period schema permits revolutionaries to represent themselves as true conservatives: they break with the recent past to renew self-conscious commitment to the principles and practices of an earlier age.

   Given the liberal's distrust of total revolution, this three-part schema is attractive. By locating at least some elements of the new order in a remoter past, liberals can suggest that they are not demanding an impossible break but a critical reappropriation of the best of a common cultural achievement. Cf. J. G. A. Pocock, *The Ancient Constitution and the Feudal Law* (1957). To glorify the perfection of past ages is silly, but I shall not allow such "golden age" exaggerations to prevent me from looking back to the remoter past to grasp the transformative possibilities of the present. See Chapters 3 and 7.

2. See Thomas Kuhn, *The Structure of Scientific Revolutions* (2d ed. 1970).

3. For another protest against totalizing conceptions of revolution, see Roberto Unger, *Social Theory: Its Situation and Its Task* 163–64 (1987). Unfortunately, Unger embeds his idea of "revolutionary reform" into a larger structure I cannot accept. Adopting an extravagantly iconoclastic ideal of personal development, he mixes irrational notions of social change and the rule of law to endorse a permanent process of "context-smashing" at all levels of social and personal

life. "Superliberalism," often described in alarmingly violent language, is what Unger calls his ideal of pervasive and ongoing disruption.

There is poetic justice, I suppose, in this act of stipulative definition. Given the willfulness of Unger's entire philosophy, why not appropriate the liberal label by an act of will? More important than his odd choice of label, Unger's emphasis on context-smashing blinds him to the importance of decisive action to consolidate revolutionary gains through constitutionalism. "Context-creation" is far more important to the revolutionary enterprise than is suggested by Unger's militantly destructive metaphors.

4. On the Jewish conception, see Michael Walzer, *Exodus and Revolution* (1985), In spite of the title, Ronald Syme's *Roman Revolution* (1939) does not enlighten the aspect of Roman understanding emphasized here. Rather than exploring the symbolic sense in which the reign of Augustus was a new beginning, Syme emphasizes the realities of oligarchic power struggle. Although the field has not fully recovered from Syme's dismissive treatment of these popular and cultural dimensions of revolutionary understanding, there are signs of reawakening. See, e.g., W. Eder, "Augustus and the Power of Tradition," in Kurt Raaflaub & Mark Tober, ed., *Between Republic and Empire* (1990). The classical Greeks were perfectly aware of sudden breaks with the past, but they were even more pessimistic than the Romans about their constructive possibilities. See Christian Meier, "Revolution in der Antike," 5 *Geschichtliche Grundbegriffe* 656–70 (1984).

5. For an insightful treatment, see Benedict Anderson, *Imagined Communities* (rev. ed. 1991).

6. See Friedrich Hayek, *Law, Legislation and Liberty* (vol. 1, 1973; vol. 2, 1976; vol. 3, 1979); Robert Nozick, *Anarchy, State, and Utopia* (1974). A more recent contribution is David Gauthier's *Morality by Agreement* (1986).

7. Thanks to the work of the last generation of liberal economists, lawyers, and policy analysts, it is increasingly difficult to sustain credibility in practical statecraft without confronting the complexities of market failure. For a useful survey, see David Weimer & Aidan Vining, *Policy Analysis: Concepts and Practice* (1989); for characteristic applications, see Charles Schulze, *The Public Use of the Private Interest* (1977); Cass Sunstein, *After the Rights Revolution* (1990).

8. See John Rawls, *A Theory of Justice* (1971).

9. See John Dewey, *Democracy and Education* (1916).

10. See Michael Walzer, *Spheres of Justice* (1983).

11. See my *Social Justice in the Liberal State* (1980) and *Reconstructing American Law* (1984).

12. The single most important polemic, Karl Popper, *The Open Society and Its Enemies*

(4th ed. 1962), is also one of the more discriminating, even supporting violent revolution under certain circumstances. See 2 id. at 151. Nonetheless, Popper's polemical purpose did not, to put it mildly, encourage him to elaborate upon the more constructive possibilities of liberal revolution.

13. The themes presented in this section are elaborated further in my book *We the People: Foundations* (1991).

14. See id.; and James Sundquist, *Dynamics of the Party System: Alignment and Realignment of Political Parties in the United States* (rev. ed. 1983).

15. Within the framework of European legal theory, a dualistic constitution may be seen as a self-revising legal order of the kind envisioned by Luhmann and Teubner. See Gunther Teubner, ed., *Autopoietic Law: A New Approach to Law and Society* (1987). In contrast to Luhmann's general tendency, I use his idea to carve out an important place for genuinely popular discussion and decision-making. Compare, e.g., Niklas Luhmann, *A Sociological Theory of Law* (trans. King-Utz and Albrow, 1985).

16. See 2 F. Hayek, supra n. 6; and his *The Road to Serfdom* (1944).

17. For a useful critique of neoconservative rhetoric, see Albert Hirschman, *The Rhetoric of Reaction: Perversity, Futility, Jeopardy* (1991).

18. See Alastair MacIntyre, *After Virtue* (2d ed. 1984); Michael Sandel, *Liberalism and the Limits of Justice* (1982). Charles Taylor, the most thoughtful contributor to this line of argument, has recently suggested doubts about its decisive character, at least when applied to the theory of the liberal state. See his *Sources of the Self* 531–32 n. 60 (1989).

19. See John Rawls, "Kantian Constructivism in Moral Theory," 77 J. Phil. 515 (1980).

20. While the stranger is a recurring figure in modern literature, he or she remains an underappreciated figure in political and legal theory. Explorations include Robert Burt, *Taking Care of Strangers* (1979); Michael Ignatieff, *The Needs of Strangers* (1986); Julia Kristeva, *Strangers to Ourselves* (1991).

3
The Next European Revolution

1. See Francis Fukuyama, *The End of History and the Last Man* (1992); Jürgen Habermas, *Die Nachholende Revolution* 171, 203 (1990). Habermas concludes his essay on the catch-up revolution by remarking that "[t]he non-Communist left has no reason to be depressed" by the events in the East (my translation). See also his downbeat "Ist der Herzschlag der Revolution auf Stillstand ge-

kommen?" in *Die Ideen von 1789*, 7, 8–16 (Forum für Philosophie Bad Homburg ed. 1989). Andrew Arato contributes an intelligent critique of the initial Western response in "Interpreting 1989," which I hope will be published soon.

2. For a social-psychological account of this dynamic, see Albert Hirschman, *Shifting Involvements* (1979); for the theory of liberal citizenship underlying it, see my *We the People: Foundations*, chs. 9–11 (1991).

3. This aspect of the comparative study of revolution is surprisingly undeveloped. For some suggestive insights, see John Dunn, *Modern Revolutions: An Introduction to the Analysis of a Political Phenomenon* (2d ed. 1989).

4. See Chapter 2; and Ackerman, supra n. 2.

5. See Alfred Cobban, *Social Interpretation of the French Revolution* (1968); François Furet, *Penser la Révolution française* (1978); J. F. Bosher, *The French Revolution* (1988). Recent work has begun to deal with the impact of the failure of the revolution upon political expectations of later generations. See, e.g., Pamela Pilbeam, *The 1830 Revolution in France* (1991).

6. Gyorgy Konrad, *Antipolitik: Mitteleuropäische Meditationen* (1985). Early on, Vaclav Havel also began to use *antipolitical* as a positive term. See his 1984 essay "Politics and Conscience," in *Open Letters: Selected Writings* 249, 269 (1991).

7. Perhaps Havel expresses this Heideggerian line most powerfully in "Politics and Conscience," supra n. 6, at 249. In "A Word about Words," in *Open Letters*, supra n. 6, at 381, Havel speaks of Heidegger as "that great genius." In "Politics and Conscience," he repeatedly presents Communism as symptomatic of a worse disease, fatal to Western liberal civilization as a whole: "I think that ... no error could be greater than the one looming largest: that of a failure to understand the totalitarian systems for what they ultimately are—a convex mirror of all modern civilization and a harsh, perhaps final call for a global recasting of how that civilization understands itself." Supra n. 6, at 259. This "ultimate" equation of "all modern civilization" with Communist totalitarianism, when joined to apocalyptic calls "for a global recasting," could, if taken seriously, lead to political blunders of Heideggerian dimension. For a recent review remarking upon Havel's "astonishingly naive, self-contradictory, and, to be frank, half-baked views in such matters," see Tony Judt, "To Live in Truth," *Times Literary Supplement* 3 (Oct. 11, 1991).

8. For example, he has repeatedly spoken out against an unduly retributive response to former Communists and collaborators with the secret police. See Chapter 5.

9. See, e.g., Jean Cohen & Andrew Arato, *Civil Society and Political Theory* (1992); Janina Frentzel-Zagorska, "Civil Society in Poland and Hungary," 42 *Soviet*

Studies 759 (1990); Krishan Kumar, "Civil Society: An Inquiry into the Usefulness of an Historical Term," *Brit. J. Soc.* (forthcoming, Autumn 1992).

10. See Chapter 1.

11. See Andrea Bonime-Blanc, *Spain's Transition to Democracy* (1987); George Gontcharof, ed., *La décentralisation*, 11 vols. (1983–88); Liesbet Hooghe, *Leap in the Dark: Nationalist Conflict and Federal Reform in Belgium* (1991).

12. To avoid foreseeable misunderstanding, let me state that I am in favor of the Maastricht accords. My only question is whether elite-managed evolutionism remains a winning strategy in the aftermath of the Cold War.

13. The mechanisms through which governments have liberated themselves from parliamentary control on both national and European levels are well described in J. H. H. Weiler, "The Transformation of Europe," 100 *Yale L.J.* 2403 (1991).

14. See Theda Skocpol, *States and Social Revolution* (1979).

4
Constitutionalizing Revolution

1. See Robert Dahl, *After the Revolution?* (1970), and Ulrich K. Preuss, *Revolution, Fortschritt und Verfassung* (1990), for insightful discussions that broadly complement the discussion presented here.

2. See, e.g., the Eastern European discussions of civil society, cited in n. 9, Chapter 3.

3. In *Democracy and the Market* 36 (1991), Adam Przeworski has a similar moment of truth. His emphasis on the strategic calculations of well-organized political elites complements my concern with the distinctive character of revolutionary movements and the symbolic significance of constitutional elaboration. I was therefore glad to see that his treatment accords with my stress on a rapidly closing window of opportunity; see id. at 87–88. As a social scientist, Przeworski is appropriately cautious, suggesting the need for testing against "systematic evidence." Given my normative focus, I believe it is more important to urge decisive action before social scientists have the opportunity to collect the necessary data.

Other recent works on "transitions to democracy" do not focus intensively on the role of constitutional formulation. Nonetheless, the interesting theoretical statement in Guillermo O'Donnell & Philippe C. Schmitter, *Transitions from Authoritarian Rule: Tentative Conclusions about Uncertain Democracies* (1986), contains some supportive insights. Reflecting upon then-recent transformations in Southern Europe and Latin America, the authors note the recurrence of a "popular upsurge" in which an insurgent coalition asserts its "identity as 'the people.'" They also suggest, for reasons like mine, that this popular mobilization will decline. Id. at 53–56. The present chapter takes their argument one more step by linking the popular upsurge more explicitly to the process of constitutional legitimation.

4. With the exception of important work by Marc Galanter, the significance of the Indian experience has not yet been adequately appreciated in comparative constitutional theory. See his *Law and Society in Modern India* (1989). Unfortunately, Galanter's work does not emphasize the questions raised here, focusing more on the Indian Supreme Court's role as a pragmatic policymaking body. Among the discussions of potential interest to comparativists, see Upendra Baxi, *The Indian Supreme Court and Politics* (1980); Gobind Das, *The Supreme Court in Quest of Identity* (1987); H. R. Khanna, *The Judiciary in India and the Judicial Process* (1985); V. R. Krishna Iyer, *Our Courts on Trial* (1987).

5. Even though the modern language of totalitarianism had not been invented, the Americans were entirely familiar with the pathological example of Cromwell, as well as the classical oppressions of Caesarism and aristocratic elitism.

6. For Madison's requests, see Madison to Washington, Letters of Dec. 7, 1786, and Dec. 24, 1786, in 2 *Writings of James Madison* 295, 300 (Hunt ed. 1901). Washington initially rejected Madison's request, claiming a conflicting engagement. Washington to Madison, Letters of Nov. 18, 1786, and Dec. 16, 1786, in 29 *Writings of George Washington* 70, 113 (Fitzpatrick ed. 1939).

7. See Robert Merton, "The Self-Fulfilling Prophecy," in *Social Theory and Social Structure* 421 (rev. ed. 1957).

8. For a useful analysis of the complex relations between arguing and bargaining, which has an application to the present problem, see Jon Elster, "Constitutionalism in Eastern Europe: An Introduction," 58 U. Chi. L. Rev. 447, 473–80 (1991). For an account of the assenting and dissenting delegates to the American convention, see Max Farrand, *The Framing of the Constitution of the United States* 194 (1913).

9. See my *We the People: Foundations*, ch. 2 (1991), and *We the People: Transformations*, ch. 2 (forthcoming).

10. Although Switzerland pioneered the referendum, early Swiss undertakings were very different from the modern plebiscite initiated by the French revolutionaries in 1793. Compare Benjamin Barber, *The Death of Communal Liberty* 170–204 (1974), with Jean-Marie Denquin, "Révolution et empire: Impératif théorique et pratique contingente," in *Référendum et plébiscite* 25–48 (1976).

11. For a discussion of the progress toward sound constitutional compromise,

see Andrzej Rapaczynski, "Constitutional Politics in Poland: A Report on the Constitutional Committee of the Polish Parliament," 58 U. Chi. L. Rev. 595 (1991). For the devastating impact of the split in Solidarity upon the elaboration of a new constitution in the Polish parliament, see id. at 602–08. Voytek Zubek provides a blow-by-blow account of the breakup between the Warsaw group of Solidarity intelligentsia and the populist group behind Walesa; see "Walesa's Leadership and Poland's Transition," Problems of Communism 69 (January–April 1991). The sad story abundantly supports Zubek's conclusion: "By cutting a deal with Walesa at the beginning of 1990, the ruling Solidarity coalition could have held together its diverse and discordant elements . . . for another year or two." Id. at 75.

12. To forestall possible misunderstanding, let me say that there is no reason why leading parliamentarians or the president himself should be barred from membership in the special convention. To the contrary, their considered judgment and final assent is essential for success; the best way to achieve their agreement may well be to involve them directly in the negotiation from the outset.

13. Both president and parliament are still debating the terms under which a constitution should be proposed and resolved—a sign that the matter is still on the agenda. In March 1992, Walesa proposed the creation of a constitutional forum of the kind advocated here. This initiative was received coolly by parliament, which is now formulating a fragmentary constitutional solution that might regulate the relations between president, government, and parliament. See "Special Reports," 1 E. Eur. Const. Rev. 9, 10 (1992). I also rely on interviews with Polish participants, who prefer to remain anonymous.

14. Poland was the only country where intellectuals and workers joined together in a sustained revolutionary movement. A small group of revolutionary intellectuals managed to survive the long haul in Czechoslovakia, but they generated little support in other social sectors. See Milan Otahal, Revolution der Intellektuellen? (forthcoming). Hungary, in turn, provides a case in which the reformist wing of the Communist party played a pivotal role, though some bottom-up elements were involved as well. See Ivan Szelenyi, "Eastern Europe in an Epoch of Transition: Toward a Socialist Mixed Economy?" in D. Stark & V. Nee, eds., Remaking the Economic Institutions of Socialism (1989). The place to begin consideration of the divergent paths taken by different Eastern European polities in the 1980s remains Timothy Garton Ash, "Does Central Europe Exist?" in The Uses of Adversity 179 (1989). See also Wiktor Osiatynski, "Revolutions in Eastern Europe," 58 U. Chi. L. Rev. 823 (1991). I comment briefly on other Eastern European developments at nn. 16, 19.

15. A country-by-country report of the constitutional situation obtaining in the spring of 1992 can be found in "Constitution Watch," 1 *E. Eur. Const. Rev.* 2 (1992).

16. In Hungary, as in Poland, the failure to take constitutional formulation seriously began with the roundtable discussions through which the insurgents gained power from the Communist regime. These culminated in agreements that were then enacted by the old legislatures as a series of amendments to the preexisting constitutions. Thus, insurgents could come to power without attempting comprehensive constitutional deliberation, let alone submission of a proposal to the People for debate and decision. For useful discussions of the individual Round Table Talks, see the following working papers submitted to the University of Chicago's Center for the Study of Constitutionalism in Eastern Europe: Wiktor Osiatynski, *The Round Table Negotiations in Poland* (1991); and Andras Sajo, *Round Tables in Hungary* (1991).

     Czechoslovakia began the process of comprehensive formulation with great energy, only to be blocked by the impasse between the Czech and Slovak parts of the federation. At that point, the retention of the old Communist constitution had an especially unfortunate effect. Formally speaking, Communist Czechoslovakia had a strong, federal constitution, which gave the Slovak minority an effective veto on all major initiatives. While Husak was in power, these paper guarantees were rendered meaningless by the centralizing structures of Communist rule. Only after the fall of Communism did the old text become important, making it easy to create a standoff between Czech and Slovak representatives in the central organs of the federation. For a thoughtful observer's view that this standoff could have been avoided by more decisive constitutional action immediately after the Velvet Revolution, see Jiri Musil, "Czechoslovakia in the Middle of Transition," 121 *Daedalus* 175, 185 (Spring 1992).

17. The figure comes from a presentation by Alexander Darchiyew, Academy of Sciences, Moscow Institute of the U.S.A. and Canada, at the Conference on Party Systems in Post-Communist Societies, held at Wissenschaftskolleg zu Berlin, Mar. 19–20, 1992.

18. For some important new work on the significance of "founding elections," see the forthcoming book by Juan Linz & Alfred Stepan, *Problems of Democratic Transition and Consolidation: Eastern Europe, Southern Europe and Latin America.*

19. The new Bulgarian Constitution was accepted only after fifty delegates from the constituent assembly walked out. These rejectionists proved exceptionally successful at the first elections under the new Constitution, whereas both the old Communist party and the non-Communists who collaborated in writing

the Constitution were set back at the polls. Presentation by Rumyana Kolarova, Sofia University, at the Conference on Party Systems in Post-Communist Societies, held at Wissenschaftskolleg zu Berlin, Mar. 19–20, 1992. This initial outcome does not augur well for the endurance of the Constitution as a symbol of political legitimacy. New constitutions are also being promulgated by the successor states to the Yugoslav Federation. Given the terrible war raging there now, it is premature to consider the extent to which these constitutions will contribute to lasting peace and a legitimate order in the region.

In spite of (because of?) the violence associated with the ouster of Ceaucescu in Romania, the old regime retains more control here than in any other country of Eastern Europe (outside the former Soviet Union). The most recent municipal elections suggest the rise of disorganized anti-Communist forces, but it is far too soon to speak of a revolution in the sense that I am using the term.

20. For example, the powers of the procuracy—an institution that grievously distorted criminal prosecution during the Communist period—are likely to survive such a superficial process of constitutional revision. Andras Sajo, "New Legalism in East Central Europe: Law as an Instrument of Social Transformation," 17 J. Law and Soc'y 329, 337 (1990).

21. On patriotic constitutionalism, see Jürgen Habermas, *Die Nachholende Revolution* 149–75 (1990).

22. Consider this assessment by Andras Sajo, one of the most thoughtful and active professors of constitutional law in Hungary: "The new Constitution was born out of a lie. It was declared to be only an amendment as the Parliament wanted to avoid the public referendum which was required for a new constitution." Sajo, supra n. 20, at 336. If this is what the liberal elites are saying, why should ordinary citizens think differently?

The leading philosopher and politician Janos Kis originally voiced skepticism about the legitimacy of the constitutional changeover in "Not without Them, Not without Us," *Uncaptive Minds* 33–34 (August–October 1989), but his doubts began to fade after his political party won a popular referendum in support of a single constitutional change modifying presidential selection procedures. "The Message of the 'Four Yeses,'" *Uncaptive Minds* 40 (January–February 1990). For a skeptical treatment of Kis's quick shift, as well as other useful orienting remarks, see Ethan Klingsberg, "Judicial Review and Hungary's Transition from Communism to Democracy: The Constitutional Court, the Continuity of Law and the Redefinition of Property Rights," *Brig. Young Univ. L. Rev.* 41, 51 n. 16 (1992).

23. For related observations, see Juan Linz, "The Perils of Presidentialism," 1 J. *Democracy* 51 (1990).

24. But perhaps this fate can be avoided by an aggressive Supreme Court? I consider this possibility in Chapter 6.

25. See Ruth Gavison, "The Controversy over Israel's Bill of Rights," 15 *Israel Yearbook on Human Rights* 113, 147–49 (1985). The story told here, confirmed by other knowledgeable observers in personal communications, goes like this. At the founding, even the religious parties actively participated in formulating the constitution "so long as they thought that there was an overwhelming majority" behind it. But then they found it possible to offer Ben-Gurion a tactical advantage: by joining with the religious parties to form a majority in the Knesset, Ben-Gurion and his supporters could avoid a coalition with the secular parties of the extreme right and the extreme left. Although this arrangement had many short-term advantages for Ben-Gurion, it meant deferring formulation of the constitution. He accepted the deal, for "[i]t was almost inconceivable for *Mapai*, Prime Minister Ben-Gurion's party, that it would one day cease being the largest single political party in Israel, and would not always serve as the basis of all government coalitions." See also my "The Lost Opportunity?" 10 *Tel Aviv University Studies in Law* 53 (1990).

26. See R. Gavison, supra n. 25, at 115–19. The Knesset has promulgated eight other segments of the Basic Law, "although constitutional scholars believe that it will be difficult to meld them into a Constitution." Id. at 119.

27. See id. at 151–54. On the weakening of ideological coherence and political solidarity, see Dan Horowitz & Moshe Lissak, *Trouble in Utopia* 245–49 (1989).

28. See Asher Arian, *Politics in Israel: The Second Generation* 86–89 (1985).

29. See "Symposium, Israel Law—Forty Years," 24 *Israel Law Review* 368, 431 (1990).

30. See Ronald Dworkin, *A Bill of Rights for Britain* (1990).

31. Relativism is a game that can be played by critics of liberalism and by its defenders. Compare John Gray, *Liberalisms: Essays in Political Philosophy* (1989), with Richard Rorty, *Contingency, Irony, and Solidarity* (1989). In both cases, relativism can be purchased only at a price. For critics of liberalism, the price is lack of philosophical depth. For defenders, it is self-satisfied celebration—as if liberalism could be identified with the West without recognizing that modern Western history reveals an unending series of sharp philosophical and practical critiques of liberal principles. Liberalism's defenders cannot simply wish these conflicts away by pretending that a consensus on fundamental values exists. We must work to build this consensus—by listening to others' objec-

tions and trying to present persuasive arguments that respond cogently to doubts.

5
The Mirage of Corrective Justice

1. I have profited from reading Jon Elster, "Retribution and Restitution: Backward-Looking Justice in Eastern Europe" (draft of March 1992); and Claus Offe, "Disqualification, Retribution, Restitution" (draft of March 1992).
2. See Guillermo O'Donnell & Philippe C. Schmitter, *Transitions from Authoritarian Rule: Tentative Conclusions about Uncertain Democracies* 28–32 (1986), for a treatment of these tensions as they have played themselves out in earlier periods.
3. See, e.g., Julia Wishnevsky, "Russians Gripped by 'Court Fever,'" 1 *RFE/RL Research Report* 1 (Mar. 6, 1992) ("Three fathers of democratic reforms in the Soviet Union—Mikhail Gorbachev, Aleksandr Yakovlev and Eduard Shevardnadze—may face trial on charges of misuse of communist party funds.")
4. See "Nächsten Mittwoch Tot," 46 *Der Spiegel* 32, 37 (Mar. 9, 1992).
5. Another recent case is provided by Greece: "When the government of Karamanlis tried to condemn some important military figures [for plainly abusive conduct during the dictatorship], it limited itself to prosecuting a few—which led to accusations 'from the other side' that it was perpetrating a 'farce' that exculpated all the others. Nevertheless, this government found itself walking a tightrope over a series of attempted coups and assassinations. [It] had considerable difficulty in applying justice to what was almost a personal clique— embarrassingly defeated in war, moreover—of middle-level officers within the Greek armed forces." O'Donnell & Schmitter, supra n. 2, at 29–30. In spite of this pessimistic assessment, O'Donnell and Schmitter support a strategy of criminal prosecution, suggesting that "if civilian politicians use courage and skill, it may not necessarily be suicidal for a nascent democracy." Id. at 32. Because the authors do not consider whether other, less "suicidal" techniques are available, I am not sure that they would hold to their judgment after making the more systematic canvass attempted in this chapter.
6. Two of the junta leaders received life sentences; the other three received terms ranging from four and a half to seventeen years. See Paula Speck, "The Trial of the Argentine Junta: Responsibilities and Realities," 18 U. *Miami Inter-Amer. L. Rev.* 491 (1986).
7. Besides the five members of the junta, it appears that only five notorious police officials were convicted. See *New York Times*, Dec. 3, 1986, sec. 1, at 3, col. 4. I have found no published suggestion that other convictions were

obtained. See, e.g., *New York Times*, June 2, 1987, sec. 1, at 20, col. 1. My estimate that forty officers were still under threat at the end of the Alfonsín regime comes from Steven Michaud, "Identifying Argentina's Disappeared," *New York Times*, Dec. 27, 1987, sec. 1, at 18, col. 1. Americas Watch listed the number as between thirty and fifty. See Juan Mendez, *Truth and Partial Justice in Argentina* 71 (1987).

For good accounts of the larger process, see Kathryn Lee Crawford, "Due Obedience and the Rights of Victims: Argentina's Transition to Democracy," 12 Hum. Rts. Q. 17 (1990); Alejandro Garro & Henry Dahl, "Legal Accountability for Human Rights Violations in Argentina: One Step Forward and Two Steps Backward," 8 Hum. Rts. L.J. 283 (1987); P. Speck, supra n. 6; Irwin Stotzky, "The Fragile Bloom of Democracy, 44 U. Miami L. Rev. 105 (1989).

8. An overall judgment on this alternative scenario would depend on the substantive content of the hypothetical Argentine constitution. If, for example, the Argentines had written a new constitution as cumbersome as the one the Brazilians came up with during the 1980s, perhaps the outcome would have been even worse than the status quo. See Keith Rosenn's excellent article "Brazil's New Constitution: An Exercise in Transient Constitutionalism for a Transitional Society," 38 Am. J. Comp. L. 773 (1990).

One thing is clear: knowledgeable Argentine commentators are increasingly willing to voice the opinion that "the trials failed to contribute to the making of a rights-based democracy." Jaime Malamud-Goti, "Punishment and a Rights-Based Democracy," *Criminal Justice Ethics* 3 (Summer–Fall 1991). Malamud-Goti does not consider whether an emphasis on constitutionalism, rather than criminality, would have been more productive in this regard. For some further thoughts on Argentina's constitutional situation, see Bruce Ackerman & Carlos Rosenkrantz, "Tres concepciones de la democracia constitucional," 29 *Cuadernos y Debates* 13 (Centro de Estudios Constitucionales, 1991).

9. The classic Supreme Court decision is *Weeks v. United States*, 232 U.S. 383 (1914). The currently fashionable instrumental objection is presented in Richard Posner, "Excessive Sanctions for Governmental Misconduct in Criminal Cases," 57 Wash. L. Rev. 635 (1982).

10. For positions broadly supporting my own, see Yale Kamisar, "Does (Did) (Should) the Exclusionary Rule Rest on a 'Principled Basis' Rather than an 'Empirical Proposition'?" 16 Creighton L. Rev. 565 (1983); Henry Henderson, "Justice in the Eighties: The Exclusionary Rule and the Principle of Judicial Integrity," 65 Judicature 354 (1982). The American position has met with a skeptical reception elsewhere—see Barry Shanks, "Comparative Analysis of

the Exclusionary Rule and Its Alternatives," 57 Tul. L. Rev. 648 (1983)—although its principled concerns have struck a responsive chord in Germany. See the decisions of the Constitutional Court at BVerfG 30, 1 (Dec. 15, 1970); BVerfG 34, 238 (Jan. 31, 1973).

11. As of June 1992, the Special Authority has about 2,200 employees, but it is growing rapidly to reach the targeted number. The governing statute is the *Stasi-Unterlagen-Gesetz*, Dec. 20, 1991 [hereinafter cited as StUG].

12. See sec. 21 of the StUG.

13. Although the governing statute guarantees all Germans access to their files, the Authority has been so overwhelmed with applications that it has so far been able to grant access only in the highest priority cases. Given the number of requests for expert opinions, the Authority does not consider it feasible to grant priority access in these cases. My description of administrative practice is based on confidential interviews with very reliable respondents both inside and outside the Authority. The description does not reflect any changes that may occur after June 1992.

14. See *Einigungsvertrag*, kap. xix, ab. iii, (4) and (5) (1990). Lower courts have begun to intervene to protect the rights of those discharged from public service. See ArbG Bonn, Urteil vom 15.11.1991—4 Ca 2074/91; ArbG Berlin, Urteil vom 4.12.1991—63A Ca 15562/91. I very much hope that this trend will be supported and expanded when similar questions reach the higher courts.

15. There seems to be surprisingly little overlap between these two categories of requests. The total number of files already requested is apparently closer to a million than it is to half a million.

16. In May 1992, there were only five fully trained lawyers on the staff.

17. Paragraph 4 of the statute does give each individual the right to submit a statement into his or her file that denies or corrects the allegations made by the Stasi. As of May 1992, only a handful of people have taken advantage of this option. Reasons for the general abstinence include the following: (1) Ordinary people do not yet have access to their files. Although the Authority will accept exculpatory statements from individuals who have not yet seen their files, people cannot readily deny or correct charges that they only imagine might be present. (2) Individuals call attention to themselves by submitting such statements to the Authority, encouraging the archivists to make a special effort to locate the material in their cases—possibly bringing forward by years the moment at which damaging information comes to the attention of the state employer.

18. To make a precise estimate of discharges will be difficult, for state employers encouraged many employees to resign to avoid the embarrassment of a formal

inquiry into their involvement with the Stasi. I have met no knowledgeable person, however, who doubts that the number of discharges is in the thousands.

19. An example is the following interview with Manfred Stolpe, whose case is described at greater length in n. 21 of this chapter: "The limit of the [Authority's] proceedings is reached the moment that it moves beyond the factual evidence and documents about an individual and tries to make value judgments. The limit is reached because the Authority is making a judgment purely on the basis of a paper record. This is a precedent that we in Brandenburg have accepted since the Prussian General Law of 1794. It was then that judgments made solely on paper records were declared insufficient and that a hearing involving the concerned parties was declared as a fundamental legal principle." "Der lange Atem der Wahrheit," 47 *Die Zeit* 3 (Apr. 17, 1992) (my translation).

20. "[Diese Arbeitsakten waren das Handwerkszeug des Stasi-Apparats.] Dass ausgerechnet da freie Phantasie walten durfte, ist unlogisch. Die Leute, die dieses Theses verbreiten, übersehen zudem, dass die Staatssicherheit sich permanent selbst kontrolliert hat. Schlampiges Arbeiten im Apparat wurde verfolgt und geahndet." "Die Akten waren das Handwerkszeug" [Interview with Joachim Gauck], 46 *Der Spiegel* 30 (Feb. 24, 1992).

21. One of these, Manfred Stolpe of Brandenburg, is currently defending himself against charges by the Special Authority that he served as an unofficial collaborator. For many years a leading legal official of the Evangelical Church in East Germany, Stolpe does not deny that he had many contacts with the Stasi. He insists, however, that they were necessary for him to protect the church and to help particular victims of oppression. His defenders point to the absence of explicit pledges of cooperation that are normally found in the files of unofficial collaborators. His accusers are not impressed; they point to evidence that they believe is incriminating, demand his resignation, and so forth.

I am in no position to judge the facts in Stolpe's case. But by the time a special parliamentary committee of the state of Brandenburg calls witnesses and reaches a decision on more evidence, Stolpe's reputation will be deeply compromised even if he is formally exculpated.

22. The Czech effort is already generating the predictable consequences. Jan Kavan, an important Czech dissident, is now accused of collaborating with the secret police while a student in Britain in 1969 and 1970: "Key portions of Mr. Kavan's 500-page secret police file have been leaked to local newspapers, although other parts were mysteriously shredded much earlier...."

With each side accusing the other of distortions, Mr. Kavan has adamantly refused to concede guilt or leave parliament, *although he said he would not run for reelection.*" *International Herald Tribune,* Apr. 14, 1992, at 2 (my emphasis). President Havel has gone along with the opening of the security files only with reluctance, and has called for amendments to laws that set the country down the German path.

23. Several people have suggested to me that it may be too late, because bits and pieces of the secret police files have already become available on the black market. Even in these cases, I think wholesale destruction of the files will eliminate most of the blackmail value of the pieces that remain. First, it will become hard to distinguish between forgeries and genuine bits. Second, blackmailers will often possess only a fragment of the relevant files, and so it will seem palpably unfair to give much credibility to the extracted bit. In contrast, German-type efforts at bureaucratization threaten to be credible enough to destroy reputations while inaccurate enough to generate an inadmissibly large number of innocent victims.

24. The current German procedures compare unfavorably to those available during the worst period of McCarthyite persecution in the United States during the 1950s—and the U.S. procedures should not provide a model for anybody. See Ralph Sharp Brown, *Loyalty and Security,* ch. 2 (1958).

25. See Joachim Gauck, *Die Stasi-Akten* (1991).

26. Some claim that it will take fifteen years before the last person gets his or her file. See "Einsicht im Jahre 2007," 46 *Der Spiegel* 47 (Mar. 16, 1992). Because every file must first be read by an official who edits it to eliminate privileged information, this estimate is not unrealistic.

27. The basic elements of the German initiative are described in Note, "Resolving Rival Claims on East German Property upon German Unification," 101 *Yale Law J.* 527 (1991).

28. The Hungarian Constitutional Court has taken the lead in emphasizing this point in the East, especially in the first of its series of land act cases. See Ethan Klingsberg, "Judicial Review and Hungary's Transition from Communism to Democracy: The Constitutional Court, the Continuity of Law and the Redefinition of Property Rights," *Brig. Young Univ. L. Rev.* 41, 81–92 (1992).

29. Although the bureaucratic staff to process these claims is being doubled from two thousand to four thousand, it is widely believed to be "unrealistic" to suppose that even a majority can be resolved in the next couple of years. See, e.g., Abine Deckwerth, "Klärung braucht Geduld," *Berliner Zeitung,* Apr. 8, 1992. In addition to the 1.2 million claims for repossession, there are about an equal number of claims for compensation, yielding a total of about 2.5

million. See, e.g., the estimate in the most recent survey of Germany, in 323 *The Economist* 11 (May 23, 1992). These published estimates are confirmed by my interviews with officials and lawyers involved in the process.

30. The six-week cutoff period is stipulated under amendments before the Bundestag at the time of this writing. See "Ansprüche der Alteigentümer können nur bis Ende 1992 angemeldet werden," *Handelsblatt* (Apr. 6, 1992). In fact, my interviews at Treuhandanstalt, the German agency charged with privatization, indicate that the agency is using existing statutory authority to allow old owners even less time to respond to development proposals made by others. This is doubtless one of the reasons why old owners have been so unsuccessful in convincing the Treuhand of the merits of their own proposals. As of June 1, the Berlin central office has processed about 240 development proposals that challenged the possessory rights of old owners. In only ten or so cases did the old owners manage to retain their possessory rights. For an introduction to the practical dilemmas confronted by the Treuhand, see Martin Keil, "Ungeklärte Eigentumsverhältnisse als praktische Probleme bei der Privatisierung von Treuhandunternehmen," 4 *Zeitschrift für Vermögens und Investitionsrecht* 121 (1992).

In spite of the remarkable success rate of developers, the existence of an ad hoc bureaucratic system will nonetheless deter development. In weighing the possible returns of embarking on a costly planning process, developers must consider the possibility that a project may be cut off by an unpredictable bureaucratic decision on behalf of the old owners. Moreover, the arbitrariness of the bureaucratic judgments will create strong incentives for corruption as competitors seek to assure a favorable decision. I should emphasize, however, that my concerns about corruption are simply theoretical at present; see Susan Rose-Ackerman, *The Economics of Corruption* (1978). Only time will tell whether Treuhand will withstand the threats to its integrity generated by existing procedures.

31. For a useful typology describing the variety of Eastern European paths to privatization, see David Stark, "Path Dependence and Privatization Strategies in East Central Europe," 6 *East Eur. Pol. & Soc.* 17 (1992). For perspectives on voucher programs, see Olivier Blanchard et al., *Reform in Eastern Europe* (1991); Andrzej Rapaczynski & Roman Frydman, "Privatization and Corporate Governance in Eastern Europe: Can a Market Economy Be Designed?" in Georg Winkler, ed., *Central and Eastern Europe: The Roads to Growth* (1992).

32. Compensation ceilings are being considered throughout Eastern Europe, but I know of no proposal that establishes the ceiling on recovery by property owners by reference to the payments granted to political prisoners.

33. Law of Oct. 4, 1991, art. 2, sec. 1 (d) (English translation on file with the author).

34. Begin with the threat of civil division: the number of informers is estimated to be "as many as 140,000." Jiri Pehe, "Parliament Passes Controversial Law on Vetting Officials," *Report on Eastern Europe* 4, 8 (Oct. 25, 1991). On bureaucratic overload: A special commission created by the statute will examine complaints by people who assert that they have been wrongly certified as "conscious collaborators" by the Federal Ministry of the Interior. It will also examine the charges of third parties who assert that the ministry has wrongly given a person a clean bill of health. The requirement imposed on third-party complaints is suitably Kafkaesque: the interlopers must put down a deposit of one thousand crowns ($40), which they will forfeit if their charges are found to be unjustified. Further review proceedings may then be invoked within the judicial system.

   As if to anticipate the crushing bureaucratic burden, the statute refuses to allow *any* complaints by persons whom the Ministry of the Interior places in other proscribed categories. These categories include not only high party officials (whose identity can readily be established) but also secret police informers whose names appear in the appropriate register. "The authorities evidently believe that there is little doubt that these people did indeed work for the secret police"—or so Pehe would have us believe. Yet apparently the ministry could put people on lists without their signing a "cooperation agreement." Pehe, supra, at 7. Because State Security procured many such agreements by threatening people with harm to themselves or their loved ones, the existence of such an agreement should not, without more evidence, permit the government to exclude a person from a management position on the ground that he or she was a spy.

35. C. Offe, supra n. 1, at 14.

36. Following the same line, it is also appropriate to adjust pensions to prevent retired members of the nomenklatura from retaining their privileged status. Officers in the secret police should not be allowed to receive high pensions while their victims continue to struggle to make ends meet.

6
Judges as Founders

1. See Laszlo Solyom, "First Year of the Constitutional Court of the Republic of Hungary" (available from the Hungarian Constitutional Court); Ethan Klingsberg, "Judicial Review and Hungary's Transition from Communism to De-

mocracy: The Constitutional Court, the Continuity of Law and the Redefinition of Property Rights," *Brigham Young Univ. L. Rev.* 41 (1992). English-language translations of the decisions mentioned in the text are also available from the court in Budapest.

2. See Michael Dobbs, "Russian Court Opens Trial of Political Corpse—Communist Party," *International Herald Tribune*, May 27, 1972, at 1 ("The new Constitutional Court of Russia rules that it has the authority to hear charges that the party . . . had violated the country's Constitution"). Carla Thorson, "Legacy of the USSR.Constitutional Supervision Committee," 1 *RFE/RL Research Report* 55 (Mar. 27, 1992), provides some useful background.

3. Nonetheless, the minor matter raised in *Marbury* generated a constitutional crisis that almost destroyed the Court's judicial independence. See James O'Fallon, "*Marbury*," 44 *Stan. L. Rev.* 219 (1992). The Court's second exercise of its power to invalidate national statutes—*Dred Scott v. Sandford*, 60 U.S. (19 How.) 393 (1857)—was instrumental in precipitating the Civil War. Although the early Court was passive in its relation with the federal government, it did intervene to impose federal norms on the states somewhat more aggressively before the Civil War.

4. Ingo Mueller, *Hitler's Justice: The Courts of the Third Reich*, chs. 22–32 (1991).

5. See Willibalt Apelt, *Geschichte der Weimarer Verfassung* 281–89 (2d ed. 1964).

6. See Donald Kommers, *The Constitutional Jurisprudence of the Federal Republic of Germany* (1989).

7. In addition to the sixty-five politicians, there were five nonvoting members from Berlin. 1 *Der Parlamentarische Rat, 1948–49: Akten und Protokolle* at xi (Wagner ed. 1975).

8. See Peter Merkl's analysis of the revealing German commentary both in and out of the assembly hall, in *The Origin of the West German Republic* 81–84 (1963).

9. The Final Communiqué of the Six-Power London Conference of June 7, 1948, began the process that ultimately yielded the Basic Law. It stipulated that "[i]f the constitution as prepared by the Constituent Assembly does not conflict with these general principles, the Military Governors will authorize its submission for ratification by the people in the respective states." 1 *Der Parlamentarische Rat*, supra n. 7, at 4.

10. Although all other West German states ratified the Basic Law, the Bavarian Landtag (parliament) expressly rejected it; instead, a majority voted to accept its validity after two-thirds of the other states had accepted it. See P. Merkl, supra n. 8, at 159. Opinion polls suggest that a referendum in Bavaria would have produced a close vote on the Basic Law. Id. at 156.

11. See id. at 53–54.

12. I am speaking only of the special ways that the revolutionary situation affects the design of judicial structures. For a thoughtful assessment of the general problem of design, see Mauro Cappelletti, *The Judicial Process in Comparative Perspective* 133–46 (1989).

13. The success of the Free Democrats in gaining an occasional seat on the Court does seem to be a function of their success in remaining within the governing coalition for long periods of time. Because this smaller party does not have nearly enough votes to deprive a candidate of the requisite two-thirds majority in the parliament, it can succeed only through negotiations with coalition partners in the government of the day.

14. For an intelligent discussion of the German selection process, see Brun-Otto Bryde, *Verfassungsentwicklung* 147–53 (1982).

15. The new Bulgarian Constitution gives the members of other high courts the power to elect four of the twelve members of the Constitutional Court. See art. 147(1). Predictably, this Constitution was devised by a constituent assembly heavily under Communist influence. See n. 19, Chapter 4.

16. See, e.g., the new constitutions promulgated in Bulgaria (see art. 150) and Romania (art. 144).

17. In fact, the great importance of ordinary citizen complaints took the West Germans by surprise. As Donald Kommers explains: "The Second Senate of the Constitutional Court [originally] decided only a handful of 'political' cases, while the First Senate was flooded with constitutional complaints and concrete review cases. As a consequence, the federal parliament amended the [relevant statute] to distribute the caseload more evenly between the senates... thus eroding the original rationale undergirding the two-senate system." See D. Kommers, supra n. 6, at 21.

18. See *Hayburn's Case*, 2 U.S. (2 Dall.) 409 (1792).

19. The classic work is Alexander Bickel, *The Least Dangerous Branch* (2d. ed. 1987).

20. L. Solyom, supra n. 1, at 3.

21. I cannot say that Solyom's conception is inconsistent with the enormous authority granted his court in its governing statute. The question is whether it is prudent to make use of power that will predictably lead to political catastrophe. Surely, it is well within the court's capacity to construe its statutory jurisdiction narrowly. Indeed, it has already done so, albeit to a very limited extent. See E. Klingsberg, supra n. 1, at 58–61.

22. See L. Solyom, supra n. 1.

23. See Constitutional Court Resolution No. 11/1992.(III.5)AB (in response to a petition submitted by the president of the republic regarding a law passed by parliament but not yet promulgated, concerning the right to prosecute

serious criminal offenses committed between Dec. 21, 1944, and May 2, 1990, that had not been prosecuted for political reasons); and Decisions No. 21/ 1990 (X.4)AB; No. 16/1991(IV.20)AB; and No. 28/1991 (VI.3)AB (relating to a series of efforts by the legislature to return property to former owners). The property decisions are discussed in Klingsberg, supra n. 1, at 87–116.

24. Although the role of the president has been the subject of a referendum, this did not cause the same wide-ranging debate as a referendum on the entire constitutional system. See Andrew Arato, "Dilemmas of the Power to Make Constitutions in Eastern Europe," at 26 (prepared for conference on comparative constitutionalism at Cardozo Law School, October 1991); see also sources cited at n. 22, Chapter 4. Certainly the role that the court has assumed has not been put up for self-conscious political approval by the electorate.

25. In addition to opinions mentioned in the text, the Court has also entered judgments in support of a right of abortion (Resolution 64/1991 (12/17/91) and has opposed the constitutionality of capital punishment (Decision 23/ 1990).

26. Article 79(3) of the Basic Law also absolutely prohibits the constitutional revision of a variety of governmental principles established by article 20. See Theodor Maunz et al., 3 *Grundgesetz: Kommentar*, art. 79(3) (1991).

27. In fact, the German Constitutional Court has been timid in making use of its ultimate weapon. See its decision in the State of Emergency Case, and especially the dissenting opinion, *Neue Juristische Wochenschrift* 275, 281 (1971). It remains unclear how much the "absolute" character of German entrenchment is merely smoke and mirrors—and a good thing, too, for clarity comes only after a severe constitutional crisis.

28. In Hungary, for example, according to the constitutional text, a single session of Parliament can amend the constitution by a two-thirds vote. In an otherwise informative and thoughtful article, Ethan Klingsberg interprets a minor amendment of the Hungarian Constitution as constituting an absolute entrenchment of fundamental rights in the manner of the Basic Law. See E. Klingsberg, supra n. 1, at 75–76. Unfortunately, I do not believe that the language of the amendment supports Klingsberg's ingenious interpretation.

29. Not surprisingly, the Hungarian Court, especially its chief justice, has increasingly found itself driven to move entirely beyond the written text and proclaim its authority to elaborate "the 'invisible constitution'—[which is] beyond the [control of both the] Constitution, which is often amended . . . [and] future Constitutions." *The Death Penalty Case*, supra n. 25, at 16. The chief justice does not describe, alas, how he expects this invisible constitution to gain the force of law without sustained popular support.

30. At this point, it may prove useful to reread the discussion of dualistic democracy presented in Chapter 1.

7
The Meaning of 1989

1. See Francis Fukuyama, *The End of History and the Last Man* (1992).

Index